THE
CAT
BOOK OF
LISTS

FACTS, FURBALLS, AND FOIBLES
FROM OUR FAVORITE FELINES

BY STEPHEN J. SPIGNESI

New Page Books
A Division of The Career Press, Inc.
Franklin Lakes, NJ

The Cat Book of Lists

Edited by Robert M. Brink

Typeset by John J. O'Sullivan

Cover design by Cheryl Cohan Finbow

Printed in the U.S.A. by Book-mart Press

To order this title, please call toll-free 1-800-CAREER-1 (NJ and Canada: 201-848-0310) to order using VISA or MasterCard, or for further information on books from Career Press.

The Career Press, Inc., 3 Tice Road, PO Box 687

Franklin Lakes, NJ 07417

www.careerpress.com

www.newpagebooks.com

Library of Congress Cataloging-in-Publication Data

Spignesi, Stephen J.
    The cat book of lists : facts, furballs, and foibles from our favorite felines / by Stephen J. Spignesi.
        p. cm.
    ISBN 1-56414-525-5 (pbk.)
    1. Cats--Miscellanea. 2. Cats--Quotations, maxims, etc. I. Title.

SF445.5 .S65 2001
636.8--dc21

                                                                2001026607

DEDICATION

This book is dedicated to my
cherished cat friends, past & present...

Bennie,

Carter,

Bandit,

Sandy,

Angel,

Poe,

Smoky,

Corky,

& Boris

ACKNOWLEDGMENTS

Special thanks to Carter Spignesi, Pam Spignesi, John White, Mike Lewis and all my fellow feline fanciers at Career Press, Kimmi Kappenberg, Gerina Dunwich, The Feline Advisory Bureau *(www.fabcats.org)*, Bruce Bender and Kensington Books, Gary Roma, the fine folks at Lick Your Chops in Branford, CT, all the library cats, all the members of *alt.cats*, *alt.animals.felines*, the SKEMERs, and the many groups that make up *rec.pets.cats*, including *rec.pets.cats-health+behavior*, and *rec.pets.cats.misc*, Dr. Edward Goglia, DVM, *Cat Fancy* magazine, Sarah Hartwell, the American Animal Hospital Association (AAHA), and *CBS.com*.

CONTENTS

INTRODUCTION

The Cat Book of Lists is a different (and categorically eclectic and eccentric) spin on the traditional "book of lists." This is my sixth "lists" book. My others are *The Odd Index, The Beatles Book of Lists, The USA Book of Lists, The Hollywood Book of Lists,* and *The UFO Book of Lists.* This particular book is more of a companion to the entire "cat experience."

Oh, yes, you will find in these pages: lists of cat trivia, cat tips, cat information, and other fun feline facts. However, you will also find articles (including a fascinating piece by Sarah Hartwell called "Cat Chat" which explains that cats do, indeed, talk); interviews (including a talk about cats with Kimmi from *Survivor*), photos (a kindle of library cats), personal memoirs, and, most uniquely, fiction and poetry!

Yes, *The Cat Book of Lists* contains reprints of such feline-focused works as the complete "Cheshire-Cat" chapter from *Alice's Adventures in Wonderland,* Edgar Allan Poe's chilling story, "The Black Cat," the Mother Goose story "Puss in Boots," the classic Rudyard Kipling short story "The Cat That Walked by Himself," and even a couple of Don Marquis's *archy and mehitabel* poems. Plus, there is information on the history of cats and even features on the big cats, animals that may be (*may* be?) the most beautiful creatures walking the earth today.

But all that aside, this book is really about one thing, and one thing only: the love we feel for our cats. This love is a genuine love, not just a fondness or mild affection. It is a pure, unadulterated love that spurs us to do whatever we can to make our cats happy, give them fulfilling lives, and make sure they are healthy. And what do we get in return?

The answer can be found in the last lines of "The End" on the Beatles' *Abbey Road* album: "And in the end, the love you take, is equal to the love you make." Our pets return our love for them with an unconditional love for us that could teach human beings a lesson or two. Our cats don't care what we look like or what we do for a living. They love us for who we are. Period.

Stephen Spignesi, proud owner of Carter and the late Bennie.

New Haven, CT

May 2001

CATS ARE BETTER THAN...

According to a December 2000 Neilsen random-dial phone survey of pet owners, people receive more joy from their pets than from the following five aspects of their lives:

- Friends
- Spiritual Life
- Sex Life
- Career
- Car

The only element of the respondents' lives that ranked higher than their pets was Family...but not by much. On a scale of 1 to 10, the "joy level" generated by family was a 9.35. Pets got an 8.55. Friends received an 8.23; Spirituality, a 7.85; Sex, a 7.35; Career, a 6.96; and their Car, a 5.88.

THE CAT FAMILY

"Felids (family Felidae) are the most carnivorous of the order Carnivora, feeding almost exclusively on vertebrate prey; they sit at the pinnacle of many food pyramids and most have few predators aside from man."

—Gillian Kerby, University of Oxford, England.

The cats that roam our homes and neighborhoods have a long and noble lineage. The modern cat can trace his lineage back to the Miocene Era of earth's prehistory—25 million years ago—and there are fossil records of very early "versions" of cats that go back 50 million years, to the Eocene Era.

There are two species of cats, and they are known and identified as the big cats and the small cats. The big cats are of the genus *Panthera*; the small cats are of the genus *Felis*.

THE BIG CATS

- Lion (*Panthera leo*)
- Tiger (*Panthera tigris*)
- Leopard (*Panthera pardus*)
- Jaguar (*Panthera onca*)
- Snow leopard (*Panthera uncia*)
- Clouded leopard (*Neofelus nebulosa*)
- Cheetah (*Acinonyx jubatus*)

THE SMALL CATS

- Lynx (*Felis lynx*)
- Bobcat (*Felis rufus*)
- Puma (*Felis concolor*)
- Wild cat (which includes Domestic cats) (*Felis sylvestris*)

- Ocelot (*Felis pardalis*)
- Black-footed cat (*Felis nigripes*)

ONE BIG DIFFERENCE BETWEEN THE BIG CATS AND THE SMALL CATS

Big cats can roar, but not purr; small cats can purr, but not roar.

Cats are of the family Felidae. There are 35 cat species in 4 individual genera. In biology's taxonomic categorizations of life forms, a family (Felidae) is below an order (Carnivora) and above a genus (which is above a species). Thus, of the big cats, a lion is of the order Carnivora, the family Felidae, the genus Panthera, and the species Leo. Of the small cats, the ocelot is of the order Carnivora, the family Felidae, the genus Felis, and the species Pardalis.

There are big and small cats on every continent and island on earth except Australia, Madagascar, and Antarctica. An exception to this is the domestic cat, which is found *everywhere* on earth. Cats can live in deserts, forests, and in the mountains. Their size ranges from 14" in length and 2.2 pounds in weight (the Black-footed cat) to 10.2' and 845 pounds (the tiger) in weight.

CHARACTERISTICS AND ABILITIES NATURAL TO BOTH THE BIG CATS AND THE SMALL CATS

- Large eyes with superior night vision.
- Large ears with a particular sensitivity to high-pitched sounds.
- A highly developed sense of smell.
- The Jacobson's organ, situated at the roof of their mouth, which enhances their senses of smell and taste.
- Facial whiskers.
- Agile climbing ability.
- A reflex which almost always allows them to land on their feet if they fall.
- Highly-developed sense of balance and orientation.
- Flexible and multi-positional super-strong neck muscles.
- Hair coats.
- They are all natural carnivores (meat-eaters).

THE LION

Lions are often illegally hunted or killed in traps set for other animals. Add to this the decreasing availability of land for lions to hunt on and their long-term survival as a species is a concern. Today, lions are only found in Africa (of course, lions can be seen in zoos all over the world) and their average life expectancy in the wild is 15 years. (They can live up to 24 years in captivity.)

- The lion is known as the "King of Beasts" because of its powerful strength and highly-developed ability to stalk and kill prey.
- Most kills for food are done by females.
- Lions may mate up to 50 times in a 24-hour period.
- It is theorized that a lion's mane is an evolutionary development to make the beast look larger and thus, frighten off predators and interlopers.
- Male lions need between 15 and 16 pounds of meat a day; females need approximately 11 pounds of meat each day.
- Lions live in prides consisting of between 1 and 6 adult males; 4 to 12 Prides stake out "their" territory, which the males patrol and guard against invaders.

THE TIGER, LEOPARD, CHEETAH, AND JAGUAR

As a group, these are some of the most magnificent animals on earth. They are all beautiful creatures, and all are highly skilled in hunting and self-preservation. Their ability to survive in the wild is, however, somewhat irrelevant, when many of these wild animals are hunted and slaughtered by man. The glorious tiger and lovely snow leopard are, unfortunately, endangered species; the cheetah and some of the other leopards are considered vulnerable; the Zanzibar leopard is now extinct.

- Tigers are only found naturally in India, Manchuria, Indonesia, and China. As with lions, though, tigers can also be found in zoos on every continent.
- A tiger's life expectancy in the wild is approximately 15 years; they can live an additional 5 years in captivity.
- Tiger's mark their territory by spraying urine and anal gland secretions on trees and rocks.
- Male tigers do not get involved in rearing their offspring.
- When a tiger lays claim to an area, he will often kill the cubs of the tiger who previously "owned" the land.
- Tigers will sometimes mate 100 times during the few days in each month in which a female is in heat.
- Tiger cubs are born blind.
- A tiger on the hunt may travel as much as 12 miles in one night in search of prey.
- Tigers need to eat almost 40 pounds of meat a day.
- Leopards are found in Africa and Southeast Asia.
- Leopards can live 12 years in the wild; 20 years in captivity.
- The "black panther" is really a black-coated leopard. (Yes, there is actually a leopard with no spots!)
- Leopards are amazing tree climbers and often carry their prey up into the branches to eat
- Leopard cubs are also born blind.
- Leopards can sleep draped over a tree branch.
- When born, a snow leopard cub's spots are completely black. They become a varied color as the cub ages.
- The biggest threat to the snow leopard's existence is man's demand for its beautiful coat.
- The Clouded leopard is part big cat, part small cat.
- The Clouded leopard is mostly found in Southern China and India, at high altitudes.
- The Clouded leopard feeds mostly on birds, monkeys, and squirrels.

- The cheetah is found in Africa, Southern Asia, and the Middle East.
- The cheetah is the fastest land-dwelling animal on earth, capable of achieving speeds of 60 miles per hour during a chase.
- Cheetahs weigh between 86 and 143 pounds and can overpower and kill animals weighing as much as 88 pounds, including gazelles, impalas, and wildebeest.
- Cheetahs eat a little over 6 pounds of meat a day.
- Cheetahs only drink every 4 days.
- Cheetah mating lasts less then 1 minute.
- Cheetah cubs are weaned off their mother when they are 3 months old, but less than a third of all cheetahs cubs survive to adulthood.
- The cheetah is the only cat whose claws are not covered by a sheath when retracted. They are always exposed and ready for either flight or attack.
- Female cheetahs deliberately avoid each other and will actually hide if they spot another female in the area.
- Cheetahs will kill other cheetahs they believe are encroaching on their territory.
- The jaguar is only found in South America.
- Jaguars are good swimmers and good "fishermen," often snaring fish from the banks by using the tip of their tail as a lure in the water.
- Jaguars will often hide and protect their killed prey by burying it.

THE SMALL CATS

There are 28 separate species of small cats on Earth, and it is good news that, so far, most of them are not endangered.

Here are the 28 small cats, followed by their population status.

- African golden cat—Not endangered
- Asiatic golden cat—Threatened
- Bay cat—Rare
- Black-footed cat—Not endangered
- Bobcat—Not endangered

- Caracal—Not endangered
- Chinese desert cat—Not endangered
- Fishing cat—Not endangered
- Flat-headed cat—Threatened
- Geoffrey's cat—Not endangered
- Jaguarundi—Threatened
- Iriomore cat—Endangered
- Jungle cat—Not endangered
- Kodkod—Not endangered
- Leopard cat—Not endangered
- Lynx—Not endangered
- Marbled cat—Not endangered
- Margay cat—Vulnerable
- Mountain cat—Rare
- Ocelot—Vulnerable
- Pallas's cat—Not endangered
- Pampas cat—Not endangered
- Puma—Not endangered
- Rusty-spotted cat—Not endangered
- Sand cat—Not endangered
- Serval—Not endangered
- Tiger cat—Vulnerable
- Wild cat—Not endangered
- Your favorite feline housecat is, yes, of the "Wild cat" species and I will leave it to you to make your own jokes about the irony of that nomenclature.

HOW TO STOP A CAT FROM SPRAYING

If you see your cat back up to a wall or door and lift its tail, the odds are it's getting ready to spray urine and mark its territory. Don't yell. Call his name, and walk over and put his tail down. This often works to stop him in his tracks. Remember, urinating is done in a squatting position; a cat stands upright when spraying, so it's fairly easy to tell when he's getting ready to spray. If you're not around when he sprays, though, then you're out of luck. Deodorizing cleaners are then the rule of order.

- All small cats rest with their paws tucked under their bodies. They all have a wrist joint that allows them to "fold down" their paws. (Big cats extend their legs out in front of them.)
- All small cats wrap their tails around their bodies when they are resting. (Big cats extend their tails out straight.)
- All small cats eat in a crouched position. (Big cats eat lying down.)
- There is a great demand for the spotted furs of some of the small cats, including the lynx, the bobcat, and the ocelot.

THE SABER-TOOTHED CAT: GONE BUT NOT FORGOTTEN

The fossil record shows that large carnivores often die out, but that their species can live on through natural selection and the evolving of smaller, more adaptable animals. This is what happened in the case of the saber-toothed cat, an enormous feline with massive, razor-sharp canines in their upper jaw.

The saber-toothed's teeth averaged 8" in length and fossils confirm that these were not used for chewing, grinding, or ripping. Their length would have made them vulnerable for breaking off, and samples of the saber-toothed's canines found in the La Brea Tar Pits in California and elsewhere are almost always intact. These teeth, instead, were used for stabbing and slashing and they were so effective that we now know that a single saber-toothed cat could take down an enormous mastodon, the ancestor of the elephant.

The saber-toothed cat walked the earth from 36.6 million years ago until about 10,000 years ago (the Oligocene through the Pleistocene epochs). Saber-tootheds were present in North America and Europe from 23.7 million years ago up to about 1.6 million years ago (the Miocene and Pliocene epochs).

Saber-tootheds evolved into killing machines: To accommodate their massive upper canines, their lower canines were greatly reduced in size; their neck muscles were thick and strong to allow the powerful and rapid downward thrust of their sabers—the killing blow—and their jaws could be opened a full 90 degree angle to allow the upper canines total access to prey.

The most recent saber-toothed cat was the Smilodon, which has been found in Europe and North America (especially California—it's their State Fossil) and which went extinct about 8,000 years B.C.

Interestingly, the fossil record shows that Smilodons suffered from arthritis and other degenerative bone diseases, as well as fractures and bone injuries, but many fossil samples also show signs of healing and recovery, indicating that injured animals were fed by pack mates and allowed to recover.

11 INTRIGUING CAT BREEDS

These cats are somewhat unusual looking. Let's just leave it at that.

Breed: The American Curl
Why it's remarkable: Its ears curl back, giving it a "devilish" look.

Breed: The Bombay
Why it's remarkable: Their fur is 100 percent black, right down to the roots.

Breed: The Cornish Rex
Why it's remarkable: It has a wavy, curly-haired short coat. In fact, even its whiskers are curly.

Breed: The Devon Rex
Why it's remarkable: It has huge ears and eyes, giving it a batlike appearance; also, its coat feels like suede.

Breed: The Japanese Bobtail
Why it's remarkable: It's got a pom-pom tail.

Breed: The Korat
Why it's remarkable: Its face is heart-shaped (the only cat with this feature); its coat is always silver-blue; its enormous eyes are always green.

Breed: The Manx

Why it's remarkable: No tail!

Breed: The Cymric

Why it's remarkable: Also no tail!

Breed: The Persian

Why it's remarkable: The most luxurious, flowing coat of the entire cat family.

Breed: The Scottish Fold

Why it's remarkable: It has folded-down ears and enormous eyes. If an owl could look like a cat, it would look like a Scottish Fold.

Breed: The Sphynx

Why it's remarkable: This cat appears hairless (even though it does have a coat of a light down, like the fur on a peach). Its body also appears to be wrinkled and many say the Sphynx's body was the inspiration for "E.T." in the Steven Spielberg movie of the same name.

CAT STATS

- **Length of gestation:** 58-69 days, conception to birth. The average is 63 days.
- **Litter size:** 1–8. The average is 4.
- **Birth weight:** 4 - 4 1/2 ounces.
- **Age of weaning:** 6-8 weeks.
- **Age kittens begin eating cat food:** 4-6 weeks.
- **Average weight of adult male cat:** 4-10 pounds.
- **Average weight of adult female cat:** 4-8 pounds.
- **Male breeding age:** 6-7 months.
- **Female breeding age:** 6-7 months.
- **Breeding span of males:** 5-7 years.
- **Breeding span of females:** 4-5 years.
- **Period of heat:** 12-15 times per year, consisting of 3-4 day cycles each time.

4 WAYS TO CALCULATE
A CAT'S AGE

*"How old would you be
if you didn't know how old you was?"*

—Satchel Paige

Over the years I have stumbled upon a wide range of systems and charts to calculate a cat's age relative to human years.

What I find most amusing about all this is the fact that we, as homo sapiens, need to know how old a cat is in our years, when, in reality, it is really nothing more than an exercise in the science of comparing apples and oranges.

A 10-year-old cat is in his 50s or 60s, but only when compared to a human lifespan. If we know that the maximum lifespan for a cat is 16 to 20 years, then it's fairly easy to understand that a 10-year-old kitty is middle-aged. Humans like to translate everything into human terms and, thus, these various systems and charts have been designed to allow us to say, "My cat is 10...but he's really 55 in human years." Being able to express a cat's age in human years is a pretty popular "hobby" these days, and here are four ways to figure it out.

These systems and charts come from a variety of sources: veterinarians, magazines, Web sites, and newspaper columns. What's most intriguing is that they're all different, thereby begging the question, do we really understand how a cat's lifespan translates into human years? My beloved feline friend Bennie died when he was 16. Knowing that he was around 80 in human years did not take away my grief, although it did comfort me by making me realize that I did a good job in caring for him and that I helped him live to what is considered a ripe old age for felines.

In the end, that's probably what these conversion charts are all about after all, right?

SYSTEM 1

(This system is the one used by the UK's Feline Advisory Bureau.)

Human Age = Cat Age	Human Age = Cat Age
6 months = 10 years	13 years = 68 years
8 months = 13 years	14 years = 72 years
1 year = 15 years	15 years = 76 years
2 years = 24 years	16 years = 80 years
3 years = 28 years	17 years = 84 years
4 years = 32 years	18 years = 88 years
5 years = 36 years	19 years = 92 years
6 years = 40 years	20 years = 96 years
7 years = 44 years	21 years = 100 years
8 years = 48 years	22 years = 104 years
9 years = 52 years	23 years = 108 years
10 years = 56 years	24 years = 112 years
11 years = 60 years	25 years = 116 years
12 years = 64 years	

SYSTEM 2

The first six months of a cat's life equals 13 years; the second six months equals 8 years; so the first year of a cat's life equals 21 human years. The second year equals 10 human years. Each subsequent year equals 3 human years. Thus:

Human Age = Cat Age	Human Age = Cat Age
6 months = 13 years	10 years = 55 years
1 year = 21 years	11 years = 58 years
2 years = 31 years	12 years = 61 years
3 years = 34 years	13 years = 64 years
4 years = 37 years	14 years = 67 years
5 years = 40 years	15 years = 70 years
6 years = 43 years	16 years = 73 years
7 years = 46 years	17 years = 76 years
8 years = 49 years	18 years = 79 years
9 years = 52 years	19 years = 82 years

SYSTEM 2, CONTINUED

Human Age = Cat Age

20 years = 85 years

21 years = 88 years

22 years = 91 years

Human Age = Cat Age

23 years = 94 years

24 years = 97 years

25 years = 100 years

SYSTEM 3

Human Age = Cat Age

1 month = 1 year

3 months = 7 years

6 months = 14 years

9 months = 18 years

1 year = 24 years

2 years = 36 years

3 years = 42 years

4 years = 45 years

5 years = 48 years

6 years = 51 years

7 years = 54 years

8 years = 57 years

Human Age = Cat Age

9 years = 60 years

10 years = 63 years

11 years = 66 years

12 years = 69 years

14 years = 75 years

15 years = 78 years

16 years = 81 years

17 years = 84 years

18 years = 87 years

19 years = 90 years

20 years = 93 years

SYSTEM 4

This system begins with 1 cat year equaling 20 human years and then each subsequent year equaling 4 human years.

Human Age = Cat Age

1 year = 20 years

2 years = 24 years

3 years = 28 years

4 years = 32 years

5 years = 36 years

6 years = 40 years

7 years = 44 years

Human Age = Cat Age

8 years = 48 years

9 years = 52 years

10 years = 56 years

11 years = 60 years

12 years = 64 years

14 years = 68 years

15 years = 72 years

SYSTEM 4, CONTINUED

Human Age = Cat Age

16 years = 76 years

17 years = 80 years

18 years = 84 years

Human Age = Cat Age

19 years = 88 years

20 years = 92 years

CATS OF ALL NATIONS

I named him Caesar,
so I could call him Julia's Caesar.

—Julia Phillips

But I tell you a cat needs a name that's particular
A name that's peculiar and more dignified
Else how can he keep up his tail perpendicular?
Or spread out his whiskers or cherish his pride?

—from "The Naming of Cats"
from *Cats: The Musical*

I subscribe to a few cat newsgroups on the Internet and in January 2001, I posted a request for cat names and hometowns for this list, which, at the time, was going to be called "Cats of America."

That title was immediately abandoned when I began receiving contributions from Australia, Germany, New Zealand, Sweden, Canada, and the United States.

Thus, "Cats of All Nations" was born and I would like to thank all the members of *alt.cats*, *alt.animals.felines*, *alt.cats.declawing-debate*, the SKEMERs (an Internet-based Stephen King fan club), and the many groups that make up *rec.pets.cats*, including *rec.pets.cats-health+behavior*, and *rec.pets.cats.misc.*, and the others.

One thing that struck me as I compiled this list was the incredible creativity evidenced in the naming of our favorite felines. If I had to pick a favorite, for sheer audacity, it would have to be "Temikah Tregleno, The Dark Carnival Kitty" from Catskill, New York. Thanks to Temikah (and, of course, her human, Jessikah).

220 OF OUR GLOBAL FELINE NEIGHBORS

- Abigail (St. Catharines, Ontario, Canada)
- Acajou (Düsseldorf, Germany)
- Aja (Mountaintop, PA)
- Akasha (Düsseldorf, Germany)
- Alexia (Malmö, Sweden)
- Alice (Brooklyn, NY)
- Angel (New Haven, CT)

- Ansel (Whitney, Ontario, Canada)
- Apiestilskin (Middletown, NY)
- Arizona (Hollidaysburg, PA)
- Arkon (Düsseldorf, Germany)
- Arty (Newton, MA)
- Asimov (Brisbane, Queensland, Australia)
- Attila the Hun (West Sacramento, CA)
- Autumn (Goshen, NY)
- Baby Doe (Brooklyn, NY)
- Bailey (Blackwood, NJ)
- Barney (Hollidaysburg, PA)
- Basil Fawlty (Adelaide, Western Australia)
- BB (Goshen, NY)
- Bea (Manassas, VA)
- Beamer (Killingworth, CT)
- Beauregard (Manassas, VA)
- Beauregard (Omaha, NE)
- Becky (Westwood, NJ)
- Bellanca (Alexandria, VA)
- Bennie and the Jets (New Haven, CT)
- Betsy (Endwell, NY)
- Big Guy (Goshen, NY)
- Blackie (Wood Dale, IL)
- Bob (New York, NY)
- Boris (Branford, CT)
- Bosley (Calgary, Alberta, Canada)
- Bruiser (Blackwood, NJ)
- Buddy (Manassas, VA)
- Buddy Jo (Hollidaysburg, PA)
- Caleb (Mystic, CT)

ANNE BROOKS

Carlotta, First Cat of New York City.

- Carlotta (New York, NY)
- Carter (New Haven, CT)
- Cassieopeia (Whitney, Ontario, Canada)
- Cato (Emerson, NJ)
- Cessie (Melbourne, Australia)
- Chance (Blackwood, NJ)
- Chandler (Brooklyn, NY)
- Charlie Chip (Hollidaysburg, PA)
- Cher (Charlottesville, VA)
- Cherokee (Moore, OK)
- Clara (Brooklyn, NY)
- Cleo (Yonkers, NY)
- Collie Cattypuss (London, England)

KAREN WOLF

Cato (right) enjoys a nap as Hobie (left) keeps watch for intruding photographers.

- Conrad (Philadelphia, PA)
- Corky (New Haven, CT)
- Crackers (San Antonio, TX)
- Creslin (Ashburn, VA)
- Cricket (Owosso, MI)
- Cybil (Dalkeith, Ontario, Canada)
- Daisy (Oakville, Ontario, Canada)
- Dax (Montpelier, VT)
- Dee Dee (Arvada, CO)
- Delenn (Ashburn, VA)
- Delilah (Auckland, New Zealand)
- Delphi (London, England)
- Denali (Mountaintop, PA)
- Dexter (Düsseldorf, Germany)
- Diamond (Hollidaysburg, PA)
- Digit (Goshen, NY)
- Diva (Wood Dale, IL)

- Django (Düsseldorf, Germany)
- Djerba (Düsseldorf, Germany)
- Djinni (Düsseldorf, Germany)
- Dora (New York, NY)
- Double-Yo-Seven, The International Cat of Mystery (Rush Springs, OK)
- Douglas Stenberg (Örebro, Sweden)
- Duncan (Brooklyn, NY)
- Felix (Malmö, Sweden)
- Finnbar (Oxford, England)
- Flash (Sterling Heights, MI)
- Flash (Sterling Heights, MI)
- Fluffernutter (Blackwood, NJ)
- Frank (Rush Springs, OK)
- George (Manassas, VA)
- Ghengis Khan (West Sacramento, CA)

STEPHEN SPIGNESI

Carter the Cat: feline paperweight.

- Gizmo (Franklin Square, NY)
- Gizmo (Owosso, MI)
- Goblin (Blackwood, NJ)
- Goblin (Houston, TX)
- Grace (New York, NY)
- Gracie (Beach Park, IL)
- Gravy (Perth, Western Australia)
- Greta Grey Cat Dutton (Auckland, New Zealand)
- Griezlie (Gent, Belgium)
- Gryphon (Whitney, Ontario, Canada)
- Gypsy (Tulsa, OK)
- Harley (Blackwood, NJ)
- Helen (Manassas, VA)
- Hobie (Emerson, NJ)
- Ivory (Sydney, Australia)
- Jack (Sydney, Australia)
- Jenüfa (Brooklyn, NY)
- Jessi (Arvada, CO)
- Jose (Espoo, Finland)
- Juliet (Melbourne, Victoria, Australia)
- Kali Kooli Kola Bud (Mountaintop, PA)
- Kato (Arvada, CO)
- Laku (Vantaa, Finland)
- Leonardo da Vinci (Adelaide, Western Australia)
- Liberty (London, England)
- Little Jake (Wood Dale, IL)
- Lucy (Annapolis, MD)
- Maboul (Gent, Belgium)
- Mackenzie (Blackwood, NJ)
- Madame Fifi (Oslo, Norway)
- MaddMaxx (Beach Park, IL)

- Madison (Blackwood, NJ)
- Majestic Wag-A-Lot Beauty, aka Beauty, aka The King of England, aka O'Beauty (Wolverhampton, England)
- Marie (Sydney, Australia)
- Marigold (Thorold, Ontario)
- Mei Ling, aka Queen Lish, aka Lilly Belle (New York, NY)
- Merriweather (Oakville, Ontario, Canada)
- Mew (Vancouver, British Columbia, Canada)
- Mikey (Endwell, NY)
- Miki (Gent, Belgium)
- Miles "Sammy" Davis Jr (Mountaintop, PA)
- Misha (Alexandria, VA)
- Mississippi (Adelaide, Western Australia)
- Missy (Savannah, GA)
- Misty (Dalkeith, Ontario, Canada)
- Molly (Annapolis, MD)
- Moloko (Sydney, Australia)
- Mongo (Arvada, CO)
- Monica (Brooklyn, NY)

HOW TO MOVE WITH A CAT

1. Keep your cat confined to one room the entire day of the move. (The bathroom, with litter and water dish, works well.)

2. Make your cat the very last thing you bring to your new place. Transport him in a carrier.

3. At your new home, place your cat in one room, with his litter, toys, and food dish, and keep him confined there until he settles down.

4. Visit him or stay with him in his room to reassure him everything's okay and then slowly let him explore his new home.

5. Do not let him wander around the new neighborhood. Either keep him confined to the yard or walk him around outside on a leash until he becomes familiar with the area.

- Moon (Montpelier, VT)
- Morris (Manassas, VA)
- Mouse (Annapolis, MD)
- Mousehole (Comox, British Columbia, Canada)
- Mr. Groucho Marx, aka Marx (Wood Dale, IL)
- Mystique (Chesterton, IN)

- Narraburra Blue Bonnie (Düsseldorf, Germany)
- Natalie (Sydney, Australia)
- Neelix (Montpelier, VT)
- Odin (Gent, Belgium)
- Odo (Franklin Square, NY)
- Opus (Arvada, CO)
- Oreo (Manassas, VA)
- Oscar (London, UK)
- Oscar the Grouch (Blackwood, NJ)
- Padme (Ashburn, VA)
- Panthria (Tulsa, OK)
- Patches (Savannah, GA)
- Patrick (Annapolis, MD)
- Pepsi (Hollidaysburg, PA)
- Persephone (Whitney, Ontario, Canada)
- Phoenix (Killingworth, CT)
- Poof! (Detroit, MI)
- Poppy (St. Albans, Hertfordshire, England)
- Purrkin's Swasi (Düsseldorf, Germany)
- Pyewackett (Manassas, VA)
- Q-tip (Bay Shore, NY)
- Rachmaninov (Rocky) (Three Bridges, NJ)
- Rascal (St. Catharines, Ontario, Canada)
- Rhythm N' Blues (Blackwood, NJ)
- Riffraff (Millbrook, NY)
- Riley (Boulder, CO)
- Ringo (New York, NY)

STEVE ROSEN

Caleb the Cat, hanging out in Mystic, Connecticut.

- Romeo (Melbourne, Victoria, Australia)
- Rommel (Gent, Belgium)
- Rufus (Calgary, Alberta, Canada)
- Sally (Manassas, VA)
- Sam (Calgary, Alberta, Canada)
- Samantha (Manassas, VA)
- Sammy, aka Samitz, aka Schmammy (New York, NY)
- Sampson (Annapolis, MD)
- Sapphire (Hollidaysburg, PA)
- Sasha (Dalkeith, Ontario, Canada)
- Scooter (Detroit, MI)
- Shalimar (Adelaide, Western Australia)

- Shawn (Blackwood, NJ)
- Sheila (Melbourne, Australia)
- Sherman, aka Chairman Miaow (Adelaide, Western Australia)
- Sierra Blue (Hollidaysburg, PA)
- Sigge (Västra Frölunda, Sweden)
- Simba (Savannah, GA)
- Smarty (Newton, MA)
- Smokey (Manassas, VA)
- Smudge (Goshen, NY)
- Smudge (London, England)
- Smulan (Västra Frölunda, Sweden)
- Snagglepuss-Billy (Jersey City, NJ)
- Sophie (Brooklyn, NY)
- Stonewall (Manassas, VA)
- Storm (Blackwood, NJ)
- Sukey (Boulder, CO)
- Surry (Tehran, Iran) ("Surry" means "yellow" in Turkish.)
- Syxx (Blackwood, NJ)
- Tabitha (Calgary, AB, Canada)
- Tafari's Abraxas (Düsseldorf, Germany)
- Taigan (Auckland, New Zealand)
- Taittinger (Perpignan, France)
- Tara (Auckland, New Zealand)
- Tasha (Yonkers, NY)
- Taz (Geneva, IL)
- Tcheeta (Gent, Belgium)
- Teemoe (Gent, Belgium)
- Temikah Tregleno, The Dark Carnival Kitty (Catskill, NY)
- Thady (Oxford, England)
- Thelma Lou (Manassas, VA)
- Thing-a-ma-jig (Goshen, NY)
- Tigger (Calgary, AB, Canada)
- Tim the Enchanter (Adelaide, Western Australia)
- Timbit (Oakville, Ontario, Canada) (A "timbit" is a Canadian doughnut hole.)
- Tinkerbell (Perpignan, France)
- Tinsel Bean (Hollidaysburg, PA)
- Titus Andronicus (Perpignan, France)
- Toe's (Goshen, NY)
- Tripod (Auckland, New Zealand)
- Unto (Espoo, Finland)
- Whisper (Detroit, MI)
- Willow (St Albans, Hertfordshire, England)
- Zanzibar (Adelaide, Western Australia)
- Ziggy Stardust (Adelaide, Western Australia)
- Zipper (Franklin Lakes, NJ)

5 JOBS FOR CAT LOVERS

*Some men are born to cats,
others have cats thrust upon them.*

—Gilbert Millstein

If you love cats to the point of wanting to work with them on a daily basis, here are five career choices right up your alley.

1. VETERINARIAN

Veterinarians are animal doctors and can either work in their own practice and animal hospital (about 30 percent of the vets in practice) or work for a vet with an established practice (most of the remainder). Vets play a major role in the health care of pets, most of which are cats and dogs, but which also includes birds, reptiles, horses, and other domesticated animals. Vets must pass a 4-year course in veterinary medicine and then be licensed to practice. Earnings range from around $35,000 for new grads to over $100,000 for established vets with their own practice. Veterinarians diagnose and treat illness, tend to injuries, do well-pet checkups and vaccinations, and euthanize terminally ill pets. Competition for admission to veterinary colleges is fierce, but it is a very rewarding career for the true animal lover.

2. VETERINARY TECHNICIAN AND VETERINARY TECHNOLOGIST

Veterinary Technicians and Veterinary Technologists perform medical tests in a laboratory environment for use in the treatment and diagnosis of diseases in animals. They also prepare vaccines

vaccines and serums for prevention of diseases, prepare tissue samples, take blood samples, and execute laboratory tests such as urinalysis and blood counts. Vet Techs also clean and sterilize instruments and materials and maintain equipment and machines. These jobs usually require an Associates Degree in Veterinary Medicine, although there is often on-the-job training as well. This is more of a technical, lab job than one in which there is a great deal of daily interaction with animals.

3. VETERINARY ASSISTANT

Veterinary Assistants are also known as Animal Caretakers, Animal Attendants, or Animal Keepers, and they feed, water, groom, bathe, and exercise animals. They also clean, disinfect, and repair their cages. Veterinary Assistants also play with the animals, provide companionship, and observe behavioral changes that could indicate illness or injury. Veterinary Assistants can find jobs in boarding kennels, animal shelters, veterinary hospitals and clinics, stables, laboratories, aquariums, and zoological parks. The

SCHOOL FOR CAT (AND OTHER ANIMAL) LOVERS

One of the most famous and acclaimed schools for veterinary technician training is the Bel-Rea Institute of Animal Technology in Denver, Colorado. Their Web site states "On completion of your veterinary technician training, you'll have skills in handling and restraining animal patients, nursing care, office procedures, anesthesia, sterilization, radiology, pharmacology, parasitology, hematology, blood chemistry and other procedures. You'll also understand basic principles of anatomy, physiology, disease processes, veterinary laboratory procedures, and surgical technique."

Bel-Rea advertises frequently on the Animal Planet cable network (there is even a link for AP on Bel-Rea's Web site) and the school also offers Internships and Financial Aid.

For further information:

Bel-Rea Institute of Animal Technology

1681 S. Dayton

Denver, Colorado 80231

(303) 751-8700

(800) 950-8001

Bel-Rea's Web site is: *www.bel-rea.com*

job duties are usually learned through on-the-job training and the pay ranges from $7 to around $11 an hour.

4. ANIMAL TRAINER

I've included Animal Trainer as a job for cat lovers because it does allow you to work with cats, but...anyone who has been around members of the family Felidae for any length of time knows that "cat" and "training" are usually mutually exclusive concepts. Cats can be "programmed"—through conditioning, rewards, and praise—to somewhat behave the way you want them to, but frankly, I think that when a cat does do something you ask him or her to do, it is just to humor you and is no guarantee of future obedience. Animal trainers either have their own business or work for a firm that trains animals, but if you go after this kind of job, expect to be working mostly with dogs.

5. PET GROOMER

Pet Groomers maintain a pet's appearance. Groomers work in pet supply stores, kennels, veterinary clinics, and animal shelters. Some Groomers operate their own grooming business. For cats, grooming involves an initial brush-out, followed by trimming the nails, cleaning the ears, a bath, and for long-hairs, a blow-dry. This job can be difficult sometimes since cats are notorious for not loving the water.

10 SECRETS OF YOUR CAT'S TAIL

Of all domestic animals the cat is the most expressive. His face is capable of showing a wide range of expressions. His tail is a mirror of his mind. His gracefulness is surpassed only by his agility. And, along with all these, he has a sense of humor.

—Walter Chandoha

I have seen an X-ray of my cat Carter's tail. When my wife and I first adopted Carter as a kitten, he was, oh, let's say, insane, for lack of a better word. Actually he was just a little "kitten manic," and was much more apt than he is now to consider inanimate objects like door knobs and table legs to be the dreaded enemy.

One day, just for the heck of it, Carter was leaping up from the floor (all 1 pound of him) to the door knob of a folding closet door. Once airborne, he would take a swing at the knob, fall back onto the carpet, eyeball the knob again (with that little ass wiggle cats make when they're getting ready to decimate something or somebody) and leap up again.

As he was indulging in this particular activity (which he obviously considered to be of great necessity and profound importance), he made a landing, let out a little kitty shriek, and immediately ran behind the vertical blinds, where he remained, panting and crying.

Uh oh, I said, and even though I did not know what he had done to himself, I knew he had gotten hurt. So I called my wife's cousin Ed. Ed is Carter's vet and has a highly regarded veterinary hospital with six vets on duty all the time. The consensus was that Carter had either injured himself somehow, or spooked himself, and I was instructed to watch him overnight and bring him in to the hospital the following morning if he was still exhibiting signs of pain. That night he slept under the piano stool, didn't eat, and cried out if I touched him in the area of his right leg.

He was no better the following day, so I brought him in and that is how I got to see an X-ray of Carter's tail. Ed sedated Carter, strapped him to an examination table belly down, and took an X-ray, which showed that Carter had broken his right hip during his strenuous gymnastics session in which he had to defend our house against the evil closet door knob.

Did you know there is no treatment for a kitten's broken hip? It heals itself (it was already beginning to knit) and we had to watch him to make sure he didn't do anything to re-injure himself, which turned out to be a fairly minor problem, since he was limping from his injury and was perfectly content to lay around and be picked up and carried. (He's no fool.)

Carter's hip healed and he has agreed to a hostile truce with door knobs, all of which he believes were responsible for his needless discomfort.

A cat's tail has between 18 and 20 vertebrae and is a barometer of feline mood. Regardless of a cat's actual position and perceived mood (lying on the couch, seemingly relaxed), its tail can speak volumes about what's really going on in that little head of his. Here is a look at 10 signals that can let you read your cat's mind...and act accordingly to shield yourself if necessary. (Those claws leave little holes that sting!)

IF YOUR CAT'S TAIL IS...

Curved, with the end twitching...

It signifies...
Annoyance or attention.

IF YOUR CAT'S TAIL IS...

Hanging down and puffed up...

It signifies...
Abject terror.

IF YOUR CAT'S TAIL IS...

Down and tucked between his legs...

It signifies...
Total submission.

IF YOUR CAT'S TAIL IS...

A figure S...

It signifies...
Relaxation and contentment.

IF YOUR CAT'S TAIL IS...

Puffed up to twice its size and curved...

It signifies...

That he is fearful, but prepared to fight.

IF YOUR CAT'S TAIL IS...

Puffed up to twice its size and straight up in the air...

It signifies...

Anger.

IF YOUR CAT'S TAIL IS...

Straight up in the air and swishing slightly...

It signifies...

A casual greeting.

IF YOUR CAT'S TAIL IS...

Straight up in the air and unmoving...

It signifies...

A highly emotional greeting.

IF YOUR CAT'S TAIL IS...

Straight up in the air but curved at the end...

It signifies...

Curiosity or excitement.

IF YOUR CAT'S TAIL IS...

Swishing rapidly from side to side...

It signifies...

Impatience, fury, serious playfulness (mock stalking), or, in some cases, DefCon 5.

30 CAT(CH) PHRASES

- **Cat burglar:** This is a slinking thief who is known for a stealthy entrance and exit from a house or apartment. You know, like a cat?

- **Cat got your tongue?:** Wassa matter? Can't put what you want to say into words?

- **A cat on a hot tin roof:** Picture a cat walking across a burning hot tin roof. Ouch, right? He'd be hopping and jumping and running in an attempt to get off the accursed surface. Describing someone as being like a "cat on hit tin roof" is saying that they are skittish, jumpy, nervous, and anxious.

- **Cat's meow:** This is used to describe something wonderful, such as an idea, a thing, or a person, as in, "Pet lovers are the cat's meow!" This is similar in message to the "cat's whiskers" and the "cat's pajamas."

- **Cat's nouns!:** This is an oath of avoidance from the 1700s, similar in meaning to "By God's wounds!"

- **Cat's pajamas:** See **"Cat's meow."**

- **Cat's whiskers:** See **"Cat's meow."**

- **Catcall:** This is a harsh or shrill whistle that is used to express derision or disapproval.

- **Cat-flat:** See **"Cat-house."**

- **Catgut:** Inferior liquor, also known as "rotgut."

- **Cat-house:** This is slang for a whorehouse or brothel.

- **Cat-house cutie:** A lady of the evening, often found in a Cat-flat or Cat-house.

- **Catnap:** Cats sleep 16 hours a day, and even when they are seemingly sound asleep, they are still on yellow alert. They are still hearing what's going on around them and they are aware of others in the room. Cats can usually awaken almost instantly and, thus, many cat watchers interpret this type of sleep state as the cat napping rather then being sound asleep. As a result, a short doze from which a human quickly awakens has become known as a catnap.

- **Catty:** Petty, spiteful, stealthy, sneaky.

- **Catwalk:** This is a narrow, elevated walkway either on a bridge or above a stage that is so thin and seemingly so precarious that only a cat could walk it safely. (But we humans do walk on them all the time.)

- **Cool cat:** Somebody too hip for words.

- **Copycat:** This refers to someone who mimics another's behavior or copies another's actions, and yet I have never understood what it had to do with cats. Cats are notoriously independent and rarely, if ever, copy other animals' behavior. One possibility might be that this refers to a kitten adapting learned behavior such as washing and grooming by watching its mother do the same things.

- **Fat cat:** A wealthy, sometimes self-indulgent person. This term is often used to describe someone that others less fortunate flatter and are obsequious to, with the hope of gaining money or favors. H. L. Mencken, writing in *The American Language*, said that it originated in 1920 and was used to describe someone who made a large campaign contribution with the hope of some eventual gain.

- **Fight like cats and dogs:** This is pretty self-explanatory if you've ever witnessed a cat and dog go at it. It's somewhat pathetic, though, to have to use this phrase to describe human beings fighting with each other, wouldn't you agree?

- **Fraidy cat:** A scaredy cat.

- **Hep cat:** See "**Cool cat.**"

- **Like something the cat dragged in:** Cats love to bring their humans "gifts." These offerings are often dead mice or birds, parts of dead mice or birds, and sometimes, still-living, yet torn-up mice or birds. These presents are usually not in too great shape, and this phrase is used to describe a human in similar condition. It goes without saying that this is not a compliment.

- **Make the fur fly:** Cause a commotion, raise a ruckus, start a fight, create turmoil, wreak havoc.

- **Pussy foot around:** Hesitate, procrastinate on a decision, skirt the issue.

- **Quick as a cat:** This one is fairly self-explanatory. Anyone who has experienced the eyeblink-quick escape of a fleeing feline through a briefly opened door can attest to just how accurate the phrase "quick as a cat' actually is!

- **Raining cats and dogs:** This unusual phrase refers to heavy downpours of rain, and its genesis is believed to be because a thunderstorm with lightning can suggest the bedlam of a cat-and-dog fight. Another explanation is that in mythological legend, dogs represented the wind and cats were believed to be able to influence the weather.

- **Rub his fur the wrong way:** What happens if you rub a cat's fur the wrong way? It annoys the cat, the fur sticks up in the air, and the act clearly goes against nature by going against the natural growth of a cat's fur. When used relative to human endeavors, this phrase refers to trying to do something against the norm or against the social compact. Parking in your boss's space, back-seat driving, or telling a mother how to discipline her children, are all acts that will rub someone's fur the wrong way and most likely cause an argument.

6 OF AESOP'S "CAT" FABLES

- The Cat and the Bat
- The Cat and the Birds
- The Cat and the Cock
- The Cat and the Mice
- The Cat and the Sparrows
- The Cat, the Monkey and the Chestnuts

- **Scaredy cat:** This is used to describe a timid, frightened person.
- **Tom cat:** This is slang for a male who has sex with many partners.
- **Who'll bell the cat?:** This comes from the Aesop's fable "The Mice in Council," which is about a group of mice who come up with the perfect plan to warn them of the approach of their nemesis, a dreaded cat who lived nearby. One of the mice came up with the idea of "belling" the cat: "If the Cat wore around her neck a little bell, every step she took would make it tinkle; then, ever forewarned of her approach, we would have time to reach our holes." All his fellow mice loved this idea, but there was one major problem with this plan: "Who'll bell the cat?" The moral of the fable is that a great plan is worthless if it is impossible to carry it out.

3 REASONS CATS RUB ON YOU (AND OTHER INANIMATE OBJECTS)

1. TO LEAVE ITS SCENT

Cats have scent glands on their forehead and on each side of their mouth and these glands secrete their specific scent. Cats will often rub against people, furniture, trees, and other "objects" that they are laying claim to. Their scent, which is detectable only to other animals (we cannot smell how we have been marked) is a signal that works as a property marker and which tells other animals to back off. What is interesting about this behavior is that it is repeated, as all cat owners know. Once is not enough and each time a cat "thinks" she owns something or wants to own something, she will rub her scent glands against the person or object's surface and reassert her claim.

2. TO SHOW AFFECTION

If you are fortunate enough to be beloved by a cat and held in high feline regard, your cat will often rub up against you while purring—even if she doesn't want to eat or play. Sometimes a cat will just have to tell you she loves you and gentle rubbing against your leg, head, or arm is one of the ways she can do this. This behavior is often accompanied by your cat's tail sticking straight up in the air, which is one more way she is telling you that you are the cat's pajamas.

3. TO GET YOUR ATTENTION

Cats have several ways of communicating to you that they want something, which, in most cases, is either food or attention (they want to play, go out, be petted, and so on.). Cats will often meow loudly to get your attention, but they will also use head butts and leg rubs as a way to get you to "listen up." Cats may not be able to speak English, but they sure know how to make us understand what they want.

41 WAYS TO SAY "CAT"

You may never need to know how to say cat in Swahili, but isn't it nice to know how anyway?

- **Arabic:** biss
- **Armenian:** gatz
- **Basque:** catua
- **Bulgarian:** kotka
- **Chinese:** mio
- **Czech:** köcka
- **Danish:** kat
- **Dutch:** kat
- **Egyptian:** mau
- **Estonian:** kass
- **Finnish:** kissa
- **French:** chat
- **German:** katze
- **Greek:** catta
- **Hawaiian:** popoki
- **Hindu:** katas
- **Icelandic:** kottur
- **Indian:** billy
- **Indonesian:** gitta
- **Italian:** gatto
- **Japanese:** neko
- **Latin:** cattus
- **Lithuanian:** katinas
- **Malay:** kucing
- **Maltese:** qattus
- **Norwegian:** katt
- **Polish:** kot
- **Portugese:** gato
- **Romanian:** pisica
- **Russian:** koshka
- **Slovak:** macka
- **Spanish:** gato
- **Swahili:** paka
- **Swedish:** katt
- **Swiss:** chaz
- **Thai:** meo
- **Turkish:** tekir
- **Ukranian:** kotuk
- **Vietnamese:** meo
- **Yiddish:** kats
- **Yugoslavian:** macka

9 SECRETS OF YOUR CAT'S BODY LANGUAGE

"...sometimes from her eyes
I did receive fair speechless messages."

—*William Shakespeare*
The Merchant of Venice

"A cat pours his body on the floor like water. It is
restful just to see him."

—*William Lyon Phelps*

Arching its back: If a cat arches its back, it is trying to make itself look much larger than it actually is, and this is usually due to a fear reflex and the cat feeling very threatened. The cat creates an inverted "U" with its body, keeps its legs straight, and its fur will often stand up and its tail puff up. All of this posturing serves to make the cat look much bigger than its actual body size and, when a cat is up against dogs or even other cats, this display will often serve to ward off an attack and allow the cat to flee safely. We have all seen a cat stand its ground when a dog or another cat challenges it. This is because the cat knows it can slice open its enemy's nose if attacked and will boldly stand tough rather than run away (which might actually trigger a hunting response from a dog or other fox). Arching its back is one of the cat's defensive tools that often works (when combined with hissing and growling) to scare away a foe before blood (and fur) is shed.

Deliberate head butts: This is usually a sign of affection and is mostly reserved for companion humans or fellows cats held in esteem by the 'butting" feline. This act also serves to mark a person with scent from the glands on the cat's forehead, warning other cats that that person or cat is "private property," so to speak.

Kneading: When a cat was a kitten, it kneaded its mother's belly to stimulate milk to flow from the mother's nipples. When it realized that this technique worked quite nicely, the activity was imprinted on the cat's brain as a good thing to remember how to do and, thus, cats knead their humans, creatures who have been known to provide food to kitty on a fairly regular basis.

53

GARY ROMA/IRON FROG PRODUCTIONS

Deml the Cat, of Pleasantville, N.Y., proves that a cat can sleep anywhere.

Nose touching: Cats will touch noses with each other as a greeting, and this is one of those instances of cat behaviors where it is obvious that cats think of us as nothing more than big cats who can provide food. Yes, cats will often touch noses with "their" humans and this act is identical in meaning to touching noses with a cat: it is a greeting and a sign of acceptance. A cat does not touch noses with a cat or person it feels threatened by. We should feel honored to touch noses with a cat. (I know I do.)

Rolling around on its back: This delightful performance activity by a cat means three things (in any or all combinations): I want to play; I trust you enough to expose my soft belly to you; I just woke up and feel like rolling around a bit before I demand to be fed, pet, or somehow given much-deserved attention. Be careful when petting a cat that is on its back, though. Although it is showing it trusts you by "offering" its soft parts to you, if you touch its belly in the wrong way, a cat may react instinctually and autonomically "rescind the invitation" and bite you to protect its belly. There is a reason cats are called a contradiction.

Slinking around: This is stalking behavior and is a rudimentary evolutionary instinct, even for indoor domesticated cats who may not have ever seen a mouse, let alone stalked one. Cats will slink around and stalk inanimate objects as part of their natural behavior, and there will also be occasions when a human's ankles (or other sensitive body parts) will transform into prey in a cat's mind and result in a bite or a scratch.

Staring: Did you ever see two cats outside, staring at each other and growling? If you stare at a cat, one of two things will happen: You will either have a fight on your hands, or the cat will look away and walk away. Cats perceive direct eye-to-eye staring as a sign of dominance that can easily escalate to a threat, and it is up to the cat as to how it chooses to react to the cat or person staring at her. If the stared-at cat feels superior to the stare-er, it will go into a defensive mode and might even lash out or attack. If a cat feels inferior and is willing to acknowledge its submissive rank to the person or cat, it will look away and walk away (although it is  also possible that a cat who feels threatened, but inferior, will attack anyway, just to protect itself). Look a cat in the eye with caution, unless you feel confident you can test the dynamic between you and the cat with no risk of life, limb, or pants leg.

Stretching: Cats stretch for the same reason humans do: It feels good. They stretch to extend their muscles after being curled up and also, when combined with rolling over on its back, to tell you it trusts you and that it wouldn't mind a stroke or two.

Washing: Cats wash even when they are not dirty. (Some humans could take a lesson from this behavior.) Cats groom themselves regularly and carefully, and they are meticulous creatures who usually cannot tolerate being soiled or unkempt in any manner. In fact, grooming and washing are so critical to a cat's general well-being that one of the first signs that a cat may not be well is an indifference to, or cessation of grooming. Washing and grooming deposits saliva on the fur which serves as a heat-regulating mechanism when it evaporates. Cats do not have sweat glands so they need to disperse body heat (especially in warmer climates) in this manner. Grooming also serves to reapply a cat's own scent to itself after it has been handled by humans, licked or rubbed up against by another cat, or it has eaten food which has left an odor on the cat's fur. According to zoologist Desmond Morris, cat grooming follows a specific, 10-step procedure:

- ✓ Lick the lips.
- ✓ Lick the side of one paw until it is wet.
- ✓ Rub the wet paw over the head, including ear, eye, cheek, and chin.
- ✓ Wet the other paw in the same way.
- ✓ Rub the wet paw over that side of the head.
- ✓ Lick front legs and shoulders.
- ✓ Lick flanks.
- ✓ Lick genitals.
- ✓ Lick hind legs.
- ✓ Lick tail from base to tip.

(See **Chapter 8** for more on a cat's body language.)

THE TOP 10 CAT BEHAVIORAL PROBLEMS

"Boy! Let your behaviour here be a credit unto them which brought you up by hand!"

—Mr. Pumblechook in *Great Expectations* by Charles Dickens

According to cat experts and the fine feline fancier folks at *Cat Fancy* magazine (who ought to know), these are the 10 most vexing problems cat owners have to deal with, in order of FAF (Feline Annoyance Factor), and some suggestions on how to deal with them.

1. LITTER BUGS

There is good reason why not using the litter box is considered the number one problem cat owners have to contend with. There is probably nothing more upsetting (or disgusting) than discovering that your beloved kitty has urinated or defecated anywhere other than in his or her litter box. (Comedian Rodney Dangerfield has a great one-liner about this problem: "I have an Egyptian cat," he tells us. "He leaves a pyramid in every room.") Because an indoor cat needs to use the litter box several times a day, this is a problem that needs to be immediately "nipped in the butt," so to speak, and the best way to stop this troublesome behavior (after you clean up, of course) is to identify why your cat is not using his litter and then correct the underlying problem.

The most common reasons cats do not go in the litter box are almost ludicrously obvious, and there are really only four: The box is dirty, the cat is sick, the cat is afraid, the cat is displeased with the accommodations. There are variations on these reasons but they are all subsets of these four.

1. YOUR CAT IS SICK.

The first thing to do is to be sure that your cat is not ill. Urinary tract infections, impacted anal glands, constipation, diarrhea, kidney troubles, and other ailments will all cause a cat to eschew his usual bathroom facilities and go whenever the urge hits and wherever he or she happens to be at the time (although sometimes cats will deliberately find a hidden spot to "make a deposit." That's always an interesting surprise when ultimately discovered.)

If your cat exhibits signs of illness such as loss of appetite, lethargy, crying as if in pain, sneezing, fever, runny eyes, or a runny nose, in addition to improper elimination, then sickness is probably the reason and you should get thy kitty to a vet asap.

2. YOUR CAT IS AFRAID.

If there has been a major change in your household (new child, new pet, new furniture with big mover guys and lots of noise, new house, apartment, roommate), then your cat is probably a nervous wreck and has decided that his usual "bathroom" is either too exposed, and that it leaves him too vulnerable and, thus, he will find another spot. The solution for this is to either eliminate the new traumatizing element (if possible, of course—you obviously cannot send back an infant or move back to your old place to calm your cat), or move the litter box to an out-of-the-way place where your cat can feel protected, safe, and private.

3. YOUR CAT HATES THE KITTY LITTER.

Have you ever been in a Stop and Shop, Wal-Mart, or Target and come upon a 12-foot high pyramid of 25-pound bags of cat litter on sale for, oh, 99¢, and thought to yourself, "Hey, a bargain!" So what if the brand isn't one you've ever heard of? For instance, "Acme Cat Litter" (yet another fine product from the company from which Wile E. Coyote buys all his anti-Road Runner stuff). Litter is litter, right?

Wrong.

Cats are creatures of habit, and they get used to certain things in their life being always the same, and that includes their cat litter. Of course many cats accept a new type of cat litter with no objections whatsoever, but sometimes a change can upset a cat and "inspire" him to find other sanitary accommodations. Usually switching types of litter within brands is not a problem. Going from Tidy Cat for Multiple Cats to Tidy Cat Immediate Odor Control, for instance, is usually tolerated quite well. They are both clay types of litter, have the same texture and general smell and most cats will not notice the difference. But switching to something like an on-sale generic litter, or from clay litter to scooping litter, or the new crystals can freak a cat out and cause problems. If you absolutely must change litter types, do it gradually, mixing the new litter with your cat's familiar litter over three litter box changes until he is finally using the new litter exclusively.

4. YOUR CAT'S LITTER BOX IS DIRTY.

The last possible cause for cat catastrophes is a dirty litter box, and there is only one person to blame for that: you. For a single indoor cat, the litter should be completely changed at least once a week. Solid waste should be scooped and flushed as soon as it is discovered or as soon as possible. (When you get home from work, for instance.) If you use clay litter, you do not scoop out urine; if you use the scoopable litter, even urine must be removed on a regular basis and flushed. If all other possible causes for your cat not using his litter box have been eliminated and a dirty box is the only remaining cause, then get on the ball and be more attentive to your cat's facilities. He or she would do the same for you, don't you think?

2. THE CLAWS CLAUSE

This is a bad one. It is extremely distressing to discover that your beloved kitty has just chewed the bejesus out of the front leg of your favorite chair or scratched up a beautiful mahogany table. Cats do this to leave their scent on an object, to sharpen their claws and shed dead claws (even if they're declawed), as a form of exercise, and to relieve stress.

If your cat is declawed then there is no harm, of course, in this scratching behavior. For those cats who still have their claws, though, there is a lot of harm in allowing this to continue and every attempt should be made to stop it in its paw tracks.

There are two basic and effective ways to prevent this kind of destructive behavior: distraction and avoidance.

Distraction involves you being there and witnessing the scratching. As soon as kitty starts to scratch something you do not want touched, you need to distract him from the action, and the best way is by startling him. An effective trick is to keep a tin can with some coins in it handy and shake it as soon as your cat starts scratching. The noise will usually frighten him and distract him from the scratching. Some experts recommend keeping a loaded water pistol handy and shooting kitty with water when he begins to scratch, but I have never liked this tactic, mainly because you always end up making a mess and wetting the furniture as well. If noise works, that's the better way to go.

Over time, kitty will begin to associate the unpleasant noise with the scratching and will probably stop scratching the furniture, but only if you recognize that he will need to displace his need to scratch furniture by scratching something else. (Nothing is going to eliminate this instinctual behavior, so get used to it.) Scratching posts are the obvious answer, and many cats easily make the transition from a sofa to a post, especially if the post is covered in the kind of material that allows him to really scratch and dig his claws into, like sisal or carpet.

There are other even simpler tricks to steer cats away from scratching furniture. I leave a 6- or 8-inch square of thick cardboard (not shirt cardboard, which is too thin) on my office floor all the time and Carter regularly uses it to scratch his declawed paws on throughout the day. He claws at the thick edge of the piece of cardboard, liking the feel of the edge against his paws. This piece of cardboard also eventually ends up with bite marks all around its perimeter, since he greatly enjoys biting on the cardboard and chewing it. You can cut a piece of this homemade scratching pad off of any standard brown cardboard shipping box and you may be amazed at how quickly your cat will begin using it.

The other trick is avoidance, which is finding a way to make the cat deliberately avoid the furniture all the time, even if you are not there to distract him. How do we do this? By making touching the furniture unpleasant to the max. No, we don't do anything to injure kitty, but we do make scratching the furniture something he will not want to do, and two-faced tape is the way.

As cat owners know, cats do not like their paw pads touched and they especially do not like the feeling of their paws sticking to something. If you cover the target piece of furniture with two-faced tape, the first time your cat touches it will be a major shock. His paw will stick to the tape and he will immediately try to pull it off. The tape will not hold him against his will, but it will register with him as something that scared him and violated his precious paws. It shouldn't take more than a few times for your cat to get the message: Paws off!

3. FIGHT CLUB

A catfight is not a pleasant event to behold. Like some furry, furious mini-Transformer, a battling feline metamorphoses into a weird mutation of a cat, one that now has fur sticking straight up in the air, a tail the size of a fez, no ears to speak of, and a teeth-baring facial expression that is basically the cat's announcement of DefCon 5.

This is not a pleasant sight, nor is it especially healthy for your cat or cats to wage war with an animal similarly equipped with the impressive (and potentially lethal) battle gear of needle-sharp teeth and razor-sharp claws.

There are two scenarios to contend with when it comes to catfights, and they are your cat fighting with a stranger, and your own cats fighting amongst themselves.

Cats can fight for a variety of reasons, with territoriality being one of the most common catalysts. If a cat feels that another cat threatens his territory or superior rank, he will often fight to defend his "homeland." This can happen inside with your own family cats or outside with cat strangers.

A woman I know adopted a kitten and named her Angel, never expecting the name to become an ironic commentary on her behavior. This woman lives on the second floor of a two-family house; her sister owns the house and lives on the first floor. Her sister has a cat named Corky.

Corky has always had the run of both floors of this house, so it was not uncommon for Corky to come upstairs the day Angel was brought home, and check out his new neighbor.

Angel had other ideas, however, since she had already decided that she was the queen of this new castle, and that no other cat should have the right to even set foot on her turf.

Corky is an older male, and he is exceptionally mellow. He sauntered in, walked up to Angel, and gave her a little investigatory, presumably welcoming sniff. Sort of a feline version of, "Hi, how are ya, pleased to meetya." Angel was having none of it, however. She arched her back, puffed up her tail, bared her fangs, and she took a lightning-quick swipe at Corky, who nonchalantly backed up a little and gave her a look as if to say, "Guess not, eh?"

If Corky had not been sent downstairs, a full-blown catfight would have definitely taken place, with little 2-pound female Angel undoubtedly being the aggressor against a male four times her size. And considering her mood, she probably would have won.

In a case like this, there is really only one solution: keep them apart, or, if you choose to let antagonistic cats "socialize," keep an eye on them at all times and watch their body language to see if either is on the verge of attacking.

Angel has since calmed down a little towards Corky (who still just sits and stares at her), but every now and then she'll take a swipe at him, obviously just to keep him in line and on his toes...er, paws.

This illustrates the critical point to remember about catfights: If one starts, it's too late.

No human is going to escape unscathed if that human is foolhardy enough to try and physically separate two warring felines. The human will become the third participant in the fight and may be bit or scratched—even to the point of needing stitches.

If the fight takes place outdoors and is between your cat and a cat stranger (usually either a neighbor's cat or a feral), you could try squirting them with a hose, which will usually scare them both off (albeit a little marinated). But, again, the best way to stop a catfight is to prevent it from starting in the first place.

As illustrated by the confrontation between Corky and Angel, special attention must be paid when your cat is outdoors and another cat shows up, close attention must be paid to the body language of both potential sparring partners. If either begins to adopt attack posturing (arched back, growling, crouching), remove your cat from the situation as soon as possible. You can try scaring off the interloper with a loud noise or by mock-chasing it, but it's best to get your kitty out of harm's way as soon as possible.

If, against your noblest efforts, a catfight begins anyway, try shouting or squirting them to end it as soon as possible. After the enemy cat leaves, most cat experts agree that you should not pick up your cat or attempt to pet it. He or she will still be in the battle zone and the reaction you get to an affectionate stroking could be a bite or a serious scratch. Veterinarians and animal psychology experts agree that the "all clear" signal will consist of your cat grooming, eating, or going to sleep. Then he or she is pretty much back to normal.

Of course, these scenarios all relate to those times when you are around. If your cat is an outdoor cat and is allowed to leave your property, then the only indication he or she was in a fight will be the visible, physical signs of the fight on your cat. By then it's too late and your feline first aid training skills may have to be called upon. (See Chapter 18.)

4. ANKLE SHE SWEET?

"Cats have intercepted my footsteps at the ankle for so long that my gait, both at home and on tour, has been compared to that of a man walking through low surf."

—Roy Blount, Jr.

At first, many new cat owners consider having their ankles attacked by their new kitty cute. "Awww, she wants to play with me." This glee soon fades after you have had your nylons ruined, suffered through bite holes and scratches on your ankles, and you almost trip and slam your head into the etagere one morning as you're leaving for work and kitty flies out of a hiding spot aimed for your feet, similar to a car darting out from a side road without even beeping its horn.

So how do we stop/prevent this hellish behavior? Simple. By outsmarting your cat. You need to pay attention to when and where this kind of attack occurs, and determine where and when kitty lies in wait for your tempting feet and ankles. Once you figure this out, carry either a catnip mouse or even a crumpled piece of paper in your hand as your walk your usual "route" and repeat your same steps. But just before you reach Ground Zero, throw the mouse or piece of paper precisely where your feet would next step. The odds are your cat will go after the toy, ignore you, and you can then make a graceful exit long before kitty looks up and says, "Hey! Where'd she go!? No fair!"

5. ENDLESS CRYING AND MEOWING

Cats almost always cry for a reason, and it's usually a very good one (at least to your cat, anyway).

Either they want food, are in pain, want attention, or feel threatened. They, therefore, want to eat, be out of pain, play, or fight and/or kill something or somebody.

Thus, if constant kitty crying or meowing is driving you up a tree, take a moment to think through the possible reasons your cat is talking to you and then decide whether you want to fulfill its need or put up with the crying.

If your cat is hungry and it's time to eat, then feed him.

If you think your cat is injured or is experiencing discomfort or pain for whatever reason, figure it out and either medicate kitty or get it to a vet. (This illustrates how important it is to always have at hand a good book on cat health care and symptoms.)

If your cat wants attention, pet him or play with him for a while until he gets bored and walks away regally, intent on lying down for a spell.

STACEY A. FARKAS

Buttons speaks his mind.

If your cat feels threatened and wants to fight, either remove the frightening person or animal from the scene, or get your cat away from the Danger Zone.

All this said, however, there is also the real possibility that your cat is just a chatterbox and absolutely none of the above applies. If that's the case with the cats in your house, either learn to live with it or walk around wearing headphones attached to a CD player.

6. RISE AND SHINE...NOW!

Even though this is considered a behavioral problem, I am of the opinion that the only reason cats act out (in this case, by insisting that you get up...now) is because they want something.

Those of you who are Stephen King fans may recall King's 1999 *Storm of the Century* miniseries in which the mysterious stranger André Linoge repeatedly told the residents of Little Tall Island, "Give me what I want and I'll go away."

This strategy works for cats, too.

Your cat torments you in the morning because he is hungry and he wants to eat, or he needs to go out, or he wants to play. So, get up and feed him or let him out, and then go back to bed. If he wants to play, throw him a crumpled up piece of paper or give him a favorite toy, although if he's waking you up in the morning, the odds are it's a meal call or bathroom call.

(And for a truly hilarious take on this particular type of wake-up call, check out Robin William's 1982 concert *An Evening with Robin Williams*, which should still be available on video. Robin, who has talked about his cats many times during his stand-up performances, describes one particularly traumatic morning when his, ahem, "Mr. Happy" was awake before he was, and his beloved kitty thought it was a toy. Ouch!)

7. AIN'T TO PROUD TO BEG

"Cats seem to go on the principle that it never does any harm to ask for what you want."

—Joseph Wood Krutch

Cats beg because they want something. It's usually something of yours, and it's usually food. Most cat owners are familiar with the feline move of standing up and putting its front paws on your leg as you're eating at the dinner table. Some owners happily give the cat a little piece of human food, be it a piece of chicken or fish or ham, or, even a little piece of pasta with tomato sauce. (I personally know several cats who have a powerful hankerin' for Italian food.)

Giving the cat some table food is usually all it takes to get a cat immediately programmed to repeatedly beg for what you are eating. Once that happens, there is no way to stop this behavior.

The only solution is to feed your cat at the same time as when you eat (and hope it is distracted enough and sated so that it will go take a bath after eating), or seclude it in another room when you sit down to eat. Some cats never beg, but most will if you all sit down to eat and the cat is in the same room. Removing the cat from the room is really the only way to prevent table begging. You cannot discipline this behavior out of a cat. In your cat's mind, it's an equation: food equals eat, so it will do everything in its power to execute that equation.

So pick a quiet room, put its litter and water dish in there, and get kitty used to being "out of town" when it's family dinnertime.

8. THE GREAT ESCAPE

This is a dangerous deed for an indoor cat, especially so if he or she has been declawed. No matter how hard you try, you are not going to discipline this behavior out of a cat.

You can try startling your cat by making a loud noise or clapping your hands if he tries to sneak out through an open door, but it will only deter him from that specific escape attempt. An open door is an irresistible temptation to a cat and it does not have be a door to the outside world. A cat confined to a single room may also try to flee through the door as soon as it is opened.

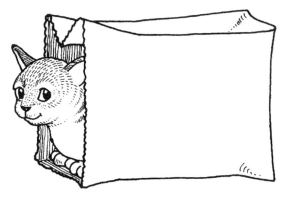

My advice: Adopt a "zero tolerance" posture for escapes. Do whatever is necessary to prevent your cat—especially your declawed cat—from running outside, even if you have to put up a barrier to create a "safe zone" where you can enter the house without leaving a clear path for kitty to use as an escape route. This is a tough problem, but if you have decided to have only indoor cats, then you must take great care to be sure that your cats stay inside, no matter what it takes to assure that.

9. SHOCKING BEHAVIOR

Chewing on electrical cords is potentially life-threatening behavior and even once can be one time too many. I remember my brother once asking me why I had all the wires in my office either under carpets, or encased in plastic tubing, or duct-taped to a cabinet or wall. It was, I told him, to make the room "Bennie-proof."

My 1981-1998 cat Bennie loved to chew on electrical wires. (Bennie was named for the Elton John song "Bennie and the Jets" even though he was a guy and the Bennie in the song was a girl. We didn't realize this little fact until it was too late and "Bennie" had been imprinted on my kitty's feline brainpan.)

(Phoenix roebelenii)
Pigmy Date Palm
tropical Asia, Africa

Some experts recommend coating exposed wires with any of a number of substances that repulse cats, such as hairspray or cayenne pepper, but I prefer hiding cords behind furniture, under carpets, runners when possible, or buying some of the aforementioned tubing to encase cords that cannot be concealed.

Lately I have seen advertised tubing products for the audio/video buff designed to consolidate and make less unsightly those tangles of electrical cords, speaker cords, connecting cords, and cables that dangle from the back of VCRs, CD/DVD players, cable boxes, etc. These products work equally well to cover electrical cords and even if your cat does decide to chew on one, he'll be chewing on thick plastic or runner and probably will not break through and chew through a wire and electrocute himself.

10. MIGHT AS WELL...JUMP!

Jumping up on tables and countertops is a behavior my wife and I personally consider completely unacceptable. If not stopped, cats will use their litter and then jump on tables and countertops where food is prepared and served. Yuck. I find this disgusting and I do not allow it in my home.

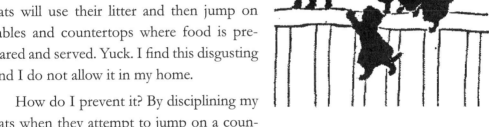

How do I prevent it? By disciplining my cats when they attempt to jump on a countertop when I am home (coins in a can, a shout, staring them in the eye and saying "No!" when you catch them), and by putting up barriers and gates to "off-limits" areas when we are not home.

To initially plant a negative reaction in your cat when he first jumps up on a table or a counter, the two-faced tape trick works well, as does laying out sheets of tin foil that they will land on when they jump up. Kitties do not like the feel of tin foil on their paws, and we've already discussed how much they hate the feel of sticky tape on their paw pads.

You can also "think like a cat" and envision the "landing spot" of the targeted area and put something there to block a "smooth landing." In my office, I go so far as to put up a screen on my desk when I am not around because I simply cannot have Carter "exploring" my computer and its wires-galore peripherals. I have found that blocking a cat's eye line often prevents them from taking that forbidden leap.

If a cat cannot see where he or she will put his little paws down, they will often think twice about making the jump, always acting as though it was their idea not to jump in the first place, of course.

🐈 🐈 🐈

Here is a list of some suggested books on cat care and understanding cat behavior:

IRON FROG PRODUCTIONS

Baker and Taylor read up on cat psychology.

- 🐈 *How To Talk To Your Cat* by Patricia Moyes (Outlet, 1993)

- 🐈 *101 Training Tips for Your Cat* by Carin A. Smith, DVM (DTP, 1994)

- 🐈 *101 Essential Tips: Cat Care* by Andrew Edney and Deni Brown (DK Publishing, 1995)

- 🐈 *The Cat's Mind: Understanding Your Cat's Behavior* by Bruce Fogle (Hungry Minds, Inc., 1995)

- 🐈 *The Cat Owner's Home Veterinary Handbook* by Delbert G. Carlson (Hungry Minds, Inc., 1995)

- 🐈 *Good Cats, Bad Habits: The Complete A-to-Z Guide for When Your Cat Misbehaves* by Alice Rhea (Fireside, 1995)

- 🐈 *Good Owners, Great Cats* by Brian Kilcommons and Sarah Wilson (Warner Books, 1995)

- 🐈 *Caring For Your Older Cat* by Chris C. Pinney (Barrons Educational Series, 1996)

- 🐈 *Cat Behavior and Training: Veterinary Advice for Owners*, Lowell Ackerman, editor (TFH Publishing, 1996)

- 🐈 *Is Your Cat Crazy? Solutions from the Casebook of a Cat Therapist* by John C. Wright and Judi Wright Lashhaits (Hungry Minds, Inc., 1996)

- 🐈 *101 Questions Your Cat Would Ask: What's Bothering Your Cat and How To Solve Its Problems* by Honor Head (Barrons Educational Series, 1999)

- 🐈 *125 Most Asked Questions About Cats (And the Answers)* by John Malone (Fine Communications, 1999)

- 🐈 *The Cat Who Cried for Help: Attitudes, Emotions, and the Psychology of Cats* by Nicholas Dodman (Bantam Doubleday Dell Publishing, 1999)

- *The Complete Idiot's Guide to a Healthy Cat* by Elaine Wexler-Mitchell (Alpha Books, 1999)
- *Cats for Dummies* by Gina Spadafori (Hungry Minds, Inc., 2000)
- *DK Handbooks: Cats* by David Alderton (DK Publishing, 2000)
- *50 Ways To Train Your Cat* by Sally Franklin (Hungry Minds, Inc., 2000)

41 EXTREMELY FAMOUS CATS

A h, cats. For almost 5,000 years they have endeared themselves to us; bewitched us; perplexed us; and amused us. We have made cats into Gods, witches, and seers.

We have also had cats wearing hats, introducing movies and TV shows, confounding us with physics puzzles, and coming back to life after being hit by a semi.

This chapter looks at 41 of the most famous felines of all time, from the Cat God Bast, to that super-cool Cat with a Hat, Top Cat.

BAST

In 1931, in his book *The Cat in the Mysteries of Religion and Magic*, M. Oldfield Howey wrote the following about the Egyptian cat goddess Bast, aka Pasht:

'As the cat sees in the darkness, so the sun, which journeyed into the underworld at night, saw through its gloom. Bast was the representative of the moon, because that planet was considered as the sun god's eye during the hours of darkness. For as the moon reflects the light of the solar system, so the cat's phosphorescent eyes were held to mirror the sun's rays when it was otherwise invisible to man. Bast as the cat-moon held the sun in her eyes during the night, keeping watch with the light he bestowed upon her, whilst her paws gripped, bruised, and pierced the head of his deadly enemy, the serpent of darkness. Thus she justified her title of tearer and render and proved it was not incompatible with love."

Bast was lion-headed before she became cat-headed. Today she is remembered mostly as a sleek black cat. Bast was the daughter of the sun God Ra and was associated with home, women's reproductive cycles, and birthing.

CATWOMAN

From DC Comics' official bio of Catwoman: "Orphaned as a girl by a suicidal mother and an alcoholic father, Selina Kyle spent time in a state home for girls before escaping an abusive headmistress to live on the streets of Gotham City. Vowing never to go hungry or wanting again, Kyle used her natural acrobatic skills and keen wits to become the most accomplished thief Gotham has ever known—a cat who walks through walls and the hands of both Gotham's finest and the Dark Knight, aka Batman."

Selina is single; 5' 7"; 125 pounds, has green eyes and black hair. Her first appearance was in *Batman* #1 in the spring of 1940. Some of Catwoman's more memorable quotes (from the 1992 *Batman Returns* movie in which Catwoman was played by Michelle Pfeiffer) include, "Life's a bitch, now so am I"; "I am Catwoman, hear me roar"; and "Who are you? Who's the man behind the bat? Maybe you can help me find the woman behind the cat." Julie Newmar was the original catwoman and still has a cult following from her time in tights (and whiskers).

The latest cinematic Catwoman is Ashley Judd who stars in a live action film scheduled (as of Fall 2001) for release in 2002.

THE CAT IN THE HAT

"We looked!/And we saw him!/The Cat in the Hat!" Dr. Seuss's *The Cat in the Hat* just might be the most popular children's book of all time. Ellen Goodman described this short book (just 220 words) as "a little volume of absurdity that work[s] like a karate chop on the weary little world of Dick, Jane, and Spot."

CHARLIE, THE LONESOME COUGAR

In this 1968 Disney adventure-comedy, Charlie the orphaned cougar was adopted as a cub by lumberman Jess and grew up happy in Jess's logging camp. Charlie's natural wildlife instincts eventually surfaced, however, and Jess found himself in a troubling situation. Wilderness wackiness ensues. Starring Ron Brown, Brian Russell, Linda Wallace, and Jim Wilson. Charlie is a wholesome family film with a lovable cat and the Disney touch.

THE CHESHIRE-CAT IN ALICE'S ADVENTURES IN WONDERLAND

Go ask Alice...

Alice first met the Cheshire-Cat in the Queen's kitchen and was immediately perplexed: The Cheshire-Cat, you see, grinned, spoke, and was able to vanish whenever he liked.

After Alice left the kitchen with the baby Pig, the Cheshire-Cat (who Alice called Cheshire-Puss, not wanting to be impolite), gave her directions to the March Hare's house, and then vanished before her eyes, starting with his tail and ending with his grin (which stayed visible for quite a time after the rest of his body had disappeared, a most disconcerting event).

Here is the chapter from Lewis Carroll's wondrous *Alice's Adventures in Wonderland* in which we—and Alice, of course—were all first introduced to this most peculiar of cats.

🐾 🐾 🐾

CHAPTER VI: PIG AND PEPPER

From *Alice's Adventures in Wonderland*
by Lewis Carroll

In which Alice meets The Cheshire Cat

For a minute or two she stood looking at the house, and wondering what to do next, when suddenly a footman in livery came running out of the wood—(she considered him to be a footman because he was in livery: otherwise, judging by his face only, she would have called him a fish)—and rapped loudly at the door with his knuckles. It was opened by another footman in livery, with a round face, and large eyes like a frog; and both footmen, Alice noticed, had powdered hair that curled all over their heads. She felt very curious to know what it was all about, and crept a little way out of the wood to listen.

The Fish-Footman began by producing from under his arm a great letter, nearly as large as himself, and this he handed over to the other, saying, in a solemn tone, "For the Duchess. An invitation from the Queen to play croquet." The Frog-Footman repeated, in the same solemn tone, only changing the order of the words a little, "From the Queen. An invitation for the Duchess to play croquet."

Then they both bowed low, and their curls got entangled together.

Alice laughed so much at this, that she had to run back into the wood for fear of their hearing her; and when she next peeped out the Fish-Footman was gone, and the other was sitting on the ground near the door, staring stupidly up into the sky.

Alice went timidly up to the door, and knocked.

"There's no sort of use in knocking," said the Footman, "and that for two reasons. First, because I'm on the same side of the door as you are; secondly, because they're making such a noise inside, no one could possibly hear you." And certainly there was a most extraordinary noise going on within—a constant howling and sneezing, and every now and then a great crash, as if a dish or kettle had been broken to pieces.

"Please, then," said Alice, "how am I to get in?"

"There might be some sense in your knocking," the Footman went on without attending to her, "if we had the door between us. For instance, if you were inside, you might knock, and I could let you out, you know." He was looking up into the sky all the time he was speaking, and this Alice thought decidedly uncivil. "But perhaps he can't help it," she said to herself; "his eyes are so very nearly at the top of his head. But at any rate he might answer questions.—How am I to get in?" she repeated, aloud.

"I shall sit here," the Footman remarked, "till tomorrow—"

At this moment the door of the house opened, and a large plate came skimming out, straight at the Footman's head: it just grazed his nose, and broke to pieces against one of the trees behind him.

"—or next day, maybe," the Footman continued in the same tone, exactly as if nothing had happened.

"How am I to get in?" asked Alice again, in a louder tone.

"Are you to get in at all?" said the Footman. "That's the first question, you know."

It was, no doubt: only Alice did not like to be told so. "It's really dreadful," she muttered to herself, "the way all the creatures argue. It's enough to drive one crazy!"

The Footman seemed to think this a good opportunity for repeating his remark, with variations. "I shall sit here," he said, "on and off, for days and days."

"But what am I to do?" said Alice.

"Anything you like," said the Footman, and began whistling.

"Oh, there's no use in talking to him," said Alice desperately: "he's perfectly idiotic!" And she opened the door and went in.

The door led right into a large kitchen, which was full of smoke from one end to the other: the Duchess was sitting on a three-legged stool in the middle, nursing a baby; the cook was leaning over the fire, stirring a large cauldron which seemed to be full of soup.

"There's certainly too much pepper in that soup!" Alice said to herself, as well as she could for sneezing.

There was certainly too much of it in the air. Even the Duchess sneezed occasionally; and as for the baby, it was sneezing and howling alternately without a moment's pause. The only things in the kitchen that did not sneeze, were the cook, and a large cat which was sitting on the hearth and grinning from ear to ear.

"Please would you tell me," said Alice, a little timidly, for she was not quite sure whether it was good manners for her to speak first, "why your cat grins like that?"

"It's a Cheshire cat," said the Duchess, "and that's why. Pig!"

She said the last word with such sudden violence that Alice quite jumped; but she saw in another moment that it was addressed to the baby, and not to her, so she took courage, and went on again:—

"I didn't know that Cheshire cats always grinned; in fact, I didn't know that cats could grin."

"They all can," said the Duchess; "and most of 'em do."

"I don't know of any that do," Alice said very politely, feeling quite pleased to have got into a conversation.

"You don't know much," said the Duchess; "and that's a fact."

Alice did not at all like the tone of this remark, and thought it would be as well to introduce some other subject of conversation. While she was trying to fix on one, the cook took the cauldron of soup off the fire, and at once set to work throwing everything within her reach at the Duchess and the baby—the fire-irons came first; then followed a shower of saucepans, plates, and dishes. The Duchess took no notice of them even when they hit her; and the baby was howling so much already, that it was quite impossible to say whether the blows hurt it or not.

"Oh, please mind what you're doing!" cried Alice, jumping up and down in an agony of terror. "Oh, there goes his precious nose"; as an unusually large saucepan flew close by it, and very nearly carried it off.

"If everybody minded their own business," the Duchess said in a hoarse growl, "the world would go round a deal faster than it does."

"Which would not be an advantage," said Alice, who felt very glad to get an opportunity of showing off a little of her knowledge. "Just think of what work it would make with the day and night! You see the earth takes twenty-four hours to turn round on its axis—"

"Talking of axes," said the Duchess, "chop off her head!"

Alice glanced rather anxiously at the cook, to see if she meant to take the hint; but the cook was busily stirring the soup, and seemed not to be listening, so she went on again: "Twenty-four hours, I think; or is it twelve? I---"

"Oh, don't bother ME," said the Duchess; "I never could abide figures!" And with that she began nursing her child again, singing a sort of lullaby to it as she did so, and giving it a violent shake at the end of every line:

"Speak roughly to your little boy,

And beat him when he sneezes:

He only does it to annoy,

Because he knows it teases."

CHORUS

(In which the cook and the baby joined): —

"Wow! wow! wow!"

While the Duchess sang the second verse of the song, she kept tossing the baby violently up and down, and the poor little thing howled so, that Alice could hardly hear the words:—

"I speak severely to my boy,

I beat him when he sneezes;

For he can thoroughly enjoy

The pepper when he pleases!"

CHORUS

"Wow! wow! wow!"

"Here! you may nurse it a bit, if you like!" the Duchess said to Alice, flinging the baby at her as she spoke. "I must go and get ready to play croquet with the Queen," and she hurried out of the room. The cook threw a frying-pan after her as she went out, but it just missed her.

Alice caught the baby with some difficulty, as it was a queer-shaped little creature, and held out its arms and legs in all directions, "just like a star-fish," thought Alice. The poor little thing was snorting like a steam-engine when she caught it, and kept doubling itself up and straightening

Lewis Carroll, author of *Alice in Wonderland.*

itself out again, so that altogether, for the first minute or two, it was as much as she could do to hold it.

As soon as she had made out the proper way of nursing it, (which was to twist it up into a sort of knot, and then keep tight hold of its right ear and left foot, so as to prevent its undoing itself,) she carried it out into the open air. "If I don't take this child away with me," thought Alice, "they're sure to kill it in a day or two: wouldn't it be murder to leave it behind?" She said the last words out loud, and the little thing grunted in reply (it had left off sneezing by this time). "Don't grunt," said Alice; "that's not at all a proper way of expressing yourself."

The baby grunted again, and Alice looked very anxiously into its face to see what was the matter with it. There could be no doubt that it had a very turn-up nose, much more like a snout than a real nose; also its eyes were getting extremely small for a baby: altogether Alice did not like the look of the thing at all. "But perhaps it was only sobbing," she thought, and looked into its eyes again, to see if there were any tears.

No, there were no tears. "If you're going to turn into a pig, my dear," said Alice, seriously, "I'll have nothing more to do with you. Mind now!" The poor little thing sobbed again (or grunted, it was impossible to say which), and they went on for some while in silence.

Alice was just beginning to think to herself, "Now, what am I to do with this creature when I get it home?" when it grunted again, so violently, that she looked down into its face in some alarm. This time there could be no mistake about it: it was neither more nor less than a pig, and she felt that it would be quite absurd for her to carry it further.

So she set the little creature down, and felt quite relieved to see it trot away quietly into the wood. "If it had grown up," she said to herself, "it would have made a dreadfully ugly child: but it makes rather a handsome pig, I think." And she began thinking over other children she knew, who might do very well as pigs, and was just saying to herself, "if one only knew the right way to change them—" when she was a little startled by seeing the Cheshire Cat sitting on a bough of a tree a few yards off.

The Cat only grinned when it saw Alice. It looked good- natured, she thought: still it had very long claws and a great many teeth, so she felt that it ought to be treated with respect.

"Cheshire Puss," she began, rather timidly, as she did not at all know whether it would like the name: however, it only grinned a little wider. "Come, it's pleased so far," thought Alice, and she went on. "Would you tell me, please, which way I ought to go from here?"

"That depends a good deal on where you want to get to," said the Cat.

"I don't much care where—" said Alice.

"Then it doesn't matter which way you go," said the Cat.

"—so long as I get somewhere," Alice added as an explanation.

"Oh, you're sure to do that," said the Cat, "if you only walk long enough."

Alice felt that this could not be denied, so she tried another question. "What sort of people live about here?"

"In that direction," the Cat said, waving its right paw round, "lives a Hatter: and in that direction," waving the other paw, "lives a March Hare. Visit either you like: they're both mad."

"But I don't want to go among mad people," Alice remarked.

"Oh, you can't help that," said the Cat: "we're all mad here. I'm mad. You're mad."

"How do you know I'm mad?" said Alice.

"You must be," said the Cat, "or you wouldn't have come here."

Alice didn't think that proved it at all; however, she went on "And how do you know that you're mad?"

"To begin with," said the Cat, "a dog's not mad. You grant that?"

"I suppose so," said Alice.

"Well, then," the Cat went on, "you see, a dog growls when it's angry, and wags its tail when it's pleased. Now I growl when I'm pleased, and wag my tail when I'm angry. Therefore I'm mad."

"I call it purring, not growling," said Alice.

"Call it what you like," said the Cat. "Do you play croquet with the Queen to-day?"

"I should like it very much," said Alice, "but I haven't been invited yet."

"You'll see me there," said the Cat, and vanished.

Alice was not much surprised at this, she was getting so used to queer things happening. While she was looking at the place where it had been, it suddenly appeared again.

"By-the-bye, what became of the baby?" said the Cat. "I'd nearly forgotten to ask."

"It turned into a pig," Alice quietly said, just as if it had come back in a natural way.

"I thought it would," said the Cat, and vanished again.

Alice waited a little, half expecting to see it again, but it did not appear, and after a minute or two she walked on in the direction in which the March Hare was said to live. "I've seen hatters before," she said to herself; "the March Hare will be much the most interesting, and perhaps as this is May it won't be raving mad—at least not so mad as it was in March." As she said this, she looked up, and there was the Cat again, sitting on a branch of a tree.

"Did you say pig, or fig?" said the Cat.

"I said pig," replied Alice; "and I wish you wouldn't keep appearing and vanish-ing so suddenly: you make one quite giddy."

"All right," said the Cat; and this time it vanished quite slowly, beginning with the end of the tail, and ending with the grin, which remained some time after the rest of it had gone.

"Well! I've often seen a cat without a grin," thought Alice; "but a grin without a cat! It's the most curious thing I ever saw in my life!"

She had not gone much farther before she came in sight of the house of the March Hare: she thought it must be the right house, because the chimneys were shaped like ears and the roof was thatched with fur. It was so large a house, that she did not like to go nearer till she had nibbled some more of the lefthand bit of mushroom, and raised herself to about two feet high: even then she walked up towards it rather timidly, saying to herself "Suppose it should be raving mad after all! I almost wish I'd gone to see the Hatter instead!"

CHURCH THE CAT IN STEPHEN KING'S "PET SEMATARY"

Churchill the cat was a sweet little kitty—until he got creamed by an 18-wheeler on the road outside his Maine home when his owner, little Ellie Creed, was away at her grandparents' house. Ellie's father Louis didn't want his daughter to have to learn too early about death and grief so he decided to take matters into his own hands. The Creeds' kindly old neighbor Jud Crandall had told Louis about a special cemetery behind the "pet sematary." This "other" burial ground was where things that were interred came back to life. So one night, Louis placed Church's dead body in a trash bag, grabbed a shovel, and went for a walk into the Maine wilderness. He buried Church in that secret cemetery and the cat did, indeed, come back to the Creeds...but he wasn't the loving pet Ellie remembered. Church had changed. And not for the better. He was mean and violent and dangerous. Did this teach Louis a lesson? Of course not, and when his son Gage was killed on the same road that claimed the life of Church, Louis once again took a night journey, with even more dire consequences as a result.

Church the cat is the most famous feline in all of Stephen King's work, in one of his most terrifying and memorable novels.

CLARENCE, THE CROSS-EYED LION

Clarence the lion had a problem with his vision (he was cross-eyed!) and so it fell on an American doctor and his family working in Africa to care for him. They took

Clarence in, turned him into a pet, and before long, Clarence was so beloved that he had his own TV series, *Daktari* —but he was still cross-eyed.

COURAGEOUS CAT

Courageous Cat starred in an animated TV series from 1963-1966. Courageous Cat was a "feline Batman" (he was created by Batman's originator Bob Kane) and CC's "Robin" was Minute Mouse. The two friends were crime fighters whose beat was Empire City (where the police chief was a dog). Some of their adventures (episodes) included *The Case of the TV Mystery, The Case of the Prehistoric Monster, The Case of the Mad Scientist, The Case of the Secret Weapon, The Case of the Monster From Outer Space, The Case of the Kidnapped Kit, The Case Of Sir Boobytrap, The Case of the Visiting Patient, The Case of the Laughing Gas Victims, The Case of the Auto Tycoons, The Case of the Undercover Agents,* and *The Case of the Flying Eye.*

THE COWARDLY LION IN "THE WIZARD OF OZ"

The Cowardly Lion, aka King of the Beasts, first appeared in the Frank Baum novel *The Wonderful Wizard of Oz,* but is best-remembered from Bert Lahr's portrayal of the character in the classic 1939 film, *The Wizard of Oz.* Over the past 60 years, thanks to the extraordinary presence of the film (it is frequently televised and available on VHS and DVD), The Cowardly Lion has become the world's favorite feline wimp, and a staunch friend to Dorothy. As The Cowardly Lion learns at the conclusion of *The Wizard of Oz,* he had within him the courage he so badly desired all along. (He didn't need a Wizard to give it to him!) Here is The Cowardly Lion's most famous speech from the movie:

"Courage! What makes a king out of a slave? Courage! What makes the flag on the mast to wave? Courage! What makes the elephant charge his tusk in the misty mist, or the dusky dusk? What makes the muskrat guard his musk? Courage! What makes the sphinx the seventh wonder? Courage! What makes the dawn come up like thunder? Courage! What makes the Hottentot so hot? What puts the "ape" in apricot? What have they got that I ain't got? Courage!"

The character of the Cowardly Lion has metamorphosed into an archetype (as have the other characters from the film: the Tin Man, and the Scarecrow) and the object lesson illustrated by the Lion's "journey" (look within, and there you will find the strength you need) still resonates today, and is one of the reasons the story has been so warmly embraced by each new generation that discovers it.

D. C. THE CAT FROM "THAT DARN CAT"

Siamese kitty D. C. ("Darn Cat") accidentally wandered into a bank robber's lair where a teller was being held hostage. The kidnapped teller manages to plant a clue on D. C. and it isn't long before a suspenseful game of hide and seek begins.

THE DREYFUS LION

This lion is the commercial mascot of the Drefyus investments firm and he appears in its ads, usually looking out quietly and stoically over the veldt. A variety of slogans, including "Lion rule," and "Rule your kingdom" then appear on the screen as the camera zooms in on the eyes of the gorgeous feline.

ELSA THE LIONESS IN "BORN FREE"

Adorable Elsa was adopted as a lion cub by Joy Adamson and her husband, Kenya game warden George Adamson, and grew to adulthood in their care. When Elsa grows up and becomes a lioness, Joy decides to educate her beloved friend as to the ways of the wild so that Elsa can ultimately live (everybody sing!) Born Free...as free as the wind blows...as free as the grass grows... Elsa and Joy's story is told in the 1966 movie *Born Free*. A TV series followed.

THE EXXON TIGER

The Exxon Tiger was introduced in 1954 as part of Standard Oil's "Put a tiger in your tank" ad campaign. Exxon discontinued using the tiger in the 1980s but created new ads in the 90s in which a cartoon Exxon Tiger roared the praises of the various convenience items sold at Exxon gas stations.

FELIX THE CAT

Remember the theme song?

"Felix the cat
The wonderful, wonderful cat
Whenever he gets in a fix,
He reaches into his bag of tricks
Felix the cat

The wonderful, wonderful cat.
You'll laugh so much,
your sides will ache
Your heart will go pit-a-pat
Watching Felix, the wonderful cat!"

Felix was a black cat with a huge smile who walked upright and often carried around a "magic bag of tricks" from which he could pull an escalator, a picnic table, or even a kangaroo. He had a hearty belly-shaking laugh and his surreal adventures delighted cartoon lovers in the sixties. Felix made his initial screen debut in the cartoon *Feline Follies* on November 9, 1919. He was extremely popular until the early 1930s, moved to comics for a period, and then starred in the successful 60s TV series bearing his name.

FRITZ THE CAT

Fritz the Cat was the creation of rebel comic artist Robert Crumb (in the magazine Comix) and Fritz's life and times was brought to the screen in 1972 in an animated, X-rated film called *Fritz the Cat* by director and screenwriter Ralph Bakshi. (A 1974 animated sequel was called *The 9 Lives of Fritz the Cat.*) The films recounted the raunchy, rebellious, irreverent, sexually explicit adventures of Fritz as he wended his way through the "happy times, heavy times" of the 1960s. *Fritz the Cat* is notable as being the first animated feature film to ever receive an X rating.

GARFIELD THE CAT

They say a cat always lands on its feet, but they don't mention the pain.
—Garfield

Garfield is a fat, lazy, egotistical feline whose favorite activity is eating and favorite food is lasagna. (Maybe he's Italian, too?) How can you not love him? His nemesis is Odie the dog and Garfield's stated goal is "world domination."

HEATHCLIFF THE CAT

Heathcliff the cat was the star of many Warner Bros. cartoon shorts in the 60s and 70s and made his feature film debut in 1986 in the (not-that-great) *Heathcliff: The Movie.* Legendary cartoonist Mel Blanc was the voice of Heathcliff.

HOBBES THE TIGER IN "CALVIN AND HOBBES"

Hobbes is a stuffed tiger who only comes to life when he's alone with his owner, young domestic terrorist, Calvin. Hobbes is wise and rational and often tries to talk Calvin out of one his many outrageous schemes and pranks. Is Hobbes a real cat? Or is he just a figment of Calvin's imagination, an alter ego to Calvin that Calvin uses to "think outside the box" (or the human)? The answer is that there is no answer. Hobbes is as real as we—and Calvin—believe him to be. Hobbes the cat was named after the 17th-century British political philosopher Thomas Hobbes, who wrote the book *Leviathan* and was a raging pessimist. Thomas Hobbes believed that human life in a "state of nature" is "solitary, poor, nasty, brutish, and short." Maybe that's why Hobbes the cat is a cat? Hobbes the philosopher certainly didn't make human life seem all that attractive.

KRAZY KAT

Krazy Kat holds the distinction of being the very first cartoon cat. He made his debut in 1910 in a comic strip bearing his name drawn by George Herriman, and six years later, in 1916, he made the move to the silver—and then, still silent—movie screen. International Film Service (a Hearst company) felt that Krazy would appeal to a wider audience if he had a foil and thus, Ignatz Mouse was born. The character of Krazy Kat was often used by Herriman as a voice for his ideological ideas and this resulted in the animated films not being as popular as they might have been if Krazy had not been so didactic. That said, though, the Krazy Kat cartoons did have over a two-decade run in the movies, and the shorts were shown continuously until 1940.

MARK TWAIN'S CATS

Mark Twain was a very serious cat lover, owned several during his life (see "Famous Cat Owners"), and had quite a lot to say about his favorite animal. Here is a sampling of his comments about cats, followed by a look at a very rare speech called "Cats and Candy" given by Twain in 1874.

MARK TWAIN'S "CAT" QUOTATIONS

"...the person that had took a bull by the tail once had learnt 60 or 70 times as much as a person that hadn't, and said a person that started in to carry a cat home by the tail was getting knowledge that was always going to be useful to him, and warn't ever going to grow dim or

doubtful. Chances are, he isn't likely to carry the cat that way again, either. But if he wants to, I say let him!"

—*Tom Sawyer Abroad*

"A home without a cat—and a well-fed, well-petted and properly revered cat—may be a perfect home, perhaps, but how can it prove title?"

—*Pudd'nhead Wilson*

"Ignorant people think it's the noise which fighting cats make that is so aggravating, but it ain't so; it's the sickening grammar they use."

—*A Tramp Abroad*

"One of the most striking differences between a cat and a lie is that a cat has only nine lives."

—*Pudd'nhead Wilson*

"A cat is more intelligent than people believe, and can be taught any crime."

—Notebook, 1895

"Of all God's creatures there is only one that cannot be made the slave of the last. That one is the cat. If man could be crossed with the cat it would improve man, but it would deteriorate the cat."

—Notebook, 1894

"By what right has the dog come to be regarded as a "noble" animal? The more brutal and cruel and unjust you are to him the more your fawning and adoring slave he becomes; whereas, if you shamefully misuse a cat once she will always maintain a dignified reserve toward you afterward—you will never get her full confidence again."

—*Mark Twain, a Biography*

"I urged that kings were dangerous. He said, then have cats. He was sure that a royal family of cats would answer every purpose. They would be as useful as any other royal family, they would know as much, they would have the same virtues and the same treacheries, the same disposition to get up shindies with other royal cats, they would be laughable vain and absurd and never know it, they would be wholly inexpensive, finally, they would have as sound a divine right as any other royal house...The worship of royalty being founded in unreason, these graceful and harmless cats

would easily become as sacred as any other royalties, and indeed more so, because it would presently be noticed that they hanged nobody, beheaded nobody, imprisoned nobody, inflicted no cruelties or injustices of any sort, and so must be worthy of a deeper love and reverence than the customary human king, and would certainly get it."

—*A Connecticut Yankee in King Arthur's Court*

"I simply can't resist a cat, particularly a purring one. They are the cleanest, cunningest, and most intelligent things I know, outside of the girl you love, of course."

—*Abroad with Mark Twain and Eugene Field*

CATS AND CANDY, BY MARK TWAIN

The following address was delivered at a social meeting of literary men in New York in 1874. I have no idea what the last line means and would welcome an explanation if anyone reading this knows what the term "had on a good ready" means.

🐈 🐈 🐈

When I was fourteen I was living with my parents, who were very poor—and correspondently honest. We had a youth living with us by the name of Jim Wolfe. He was an excellent fellow, seventeen years old, and very diffident. He and I slept together—virtuously; and one bitter winter's night a cousin Mary—she's married now and gone—gave what they call a candy-pulling in those days in the West, and they took the saucers of hot candy outside of the house into the snow, under a sort of old bower that came from the eaves—it was a sort of an ell then, all covered with vines—to cool this hot candy in the snow, and they were all sitting there. In the mean time we were gone to bed. We were not invited to attend this party; we were too young.

The young ladies and gentlemen were assembled there, and Jim and I were in bed. There was about four inches of snow on the roof of this ell, and our windows looked out on it; and it was frozen hard. A couple of tomcats—it is possible one might have been of the opposite sex—were assembled on the chimney in the middle of this ell, and they were growling at a fearful rate, and switching their tails about and going on, and we couldn't sleep at all.

Finally Jim said, "For two cents I'd go out and snake them cats off that chimney." So I said, "Of course you would." He said, "Well, I would; I have a mighty good notion to do it." Says I, "Of course you have; certainly you have, you have a great notion to do it." I hoped he might try it, but I was afraid he wouldn't.

Finally I did get his ambition up, and he raised the window and climbed out on the icy roof, with nothing on but his socks and a very short shirt. He went climbing along on all fours on the roof toward the chimney where the cats were. In the mean time these young ladies and gentlemen were enjoying themselves down under the eaves, and when Jim got almost to that chimney he made a pass at the cats, and his heels flew up and he shot down and crashed through those vines, and lit in the midst of the ladies and gentlemen, and sat down in those hot saucers of candy.

There was a stampede, of course, and he came up-stairs dropping pieces of chinaware and candy all the way up, and when he got up there—now anybody in the world would have gone into profanity or something calculated to relieve the mind, but he didn't; he scraped the candy off his legs, nursed his blisters a little, and said, "I could have ketched them cats if I had had on a good ready."

MEHITABEL THE ALLEY CAT IN "ARCHY AND MEHITABEL"

The archy and mehitabel poems first appeared in 1927. They were written by *New York Tribune* humorist Donald "Don" Marquis and told the stories of a cockroach named archy (who was the reincarnation of a poet) and his pet alley cat mehitabel (who was the reincarnation of Cleopatra...not Cleopatra's cat, but Cleopatra herself). As a forerunner of the equally horny Fritz the Cat, mehitabel had a series of rowdy misadventures and raunchy escapades. Here is the first stanza of one of the most popular of the archy and mehitabel poems, "the song of mehitabel." (Following this archy and mehitabel excerpt is another Don Marquis "cat" poem (albeit a non archy and mehitabel poem) that we thought you might find interesting.)

🐈 🐈 🐈

the song of mehitabel
this is the song of mehitabel
of mehitabel the alley cat
as i wrote you before boss
mehitabel is a believer
in the pythagorean
theory of the transmigration
of the soul and she claims
that formerly her spirit
was incarnated in the body
of cleopatra

I WAS CLEOPATRA ONCE
SHE SAID.

that was a long time ago
and one must not be
surprised if mehitabel
has forgotten some of her
more regal manners

The Tom Cat

At midnight in the alley
A Tom-cat comes to wail,
And he chants the hate of a million years
As he swings his snaky tail.
Malevolent, bony, brindled,
Tiger and devil and bard,
His eyes are coals from the middle of Hell
And his heart is black and hard.
He twists and crouches and capers
And bares his curved sharp claws,
And he sings to the stars of the jungle nights,
Ere cities were, or laws.
Beasts from a world primeval,
He and his leaping clan,
When the blotched red moon leers over the roofs,

READS IT AND
SNIFFS AT IT.

Give voice to their scorn of man.
He will lie on a rug tomorrow
And lick his silky fur,
And veil the brute in his yellow eyes
And play he's tame, and purr.
But at midnight in the alley
He will crouch again and wail,
And beat the time for his demon's song.
With the swing of his demon's tail.

THE MGM LION

Didn't you always feel a frisson of anticipation whenever this big beautiful lion let out a roar before every MGM movie began? Who was he? He was Leo the lion, and he was owned by animal trainer Volney Phifer, who taught him how to roar on cue. Leo died in 1936 in Gillette, New Jersey, at Phifer's home, and that is where he is buried in Phifer's front yard. Phifer placed a granite block on Leo's grave, which was removed by the new owner of the property in 1996. A pine tree planted above Leo's grave still stands and, reportedly, the current owner plans to have the tree carved into the figure of a lion when he can afford it. The Grave of Leo the Lion can be found on the northbound side of Morristown Road in Gillette, New Jersey, about a half mile north of Valley Road, just south of the railroad tracks.

MICHAEL JACKSON AS A PANTHER IN THE "BLACK OR WHITE" VIDEO

Michael morphs! Michael Jackson's 1991 John Landis-directed music video *Black or White* was revolutionary for its time, in that it made amazing use of the then-still relatively new special effect technique of morphing. (And expensive. Reportedly the special effects budget alone for the video ran close to $1 million a minute.) Today, morphing—a fluid transformation from one image to another, seemingly in one flowing sequence—is commonplace in videos, TV commercials, and movies, but at the time, *Black or White* was groundbreaking. That said, though, there is no denying that this video—in its original incarnation—is mega-weird.

The video, which debuted simultaneously on FOX, MTV, and BET, begins with George Wendt as a dad yelling at his son (played by Jackson pal McCauley Culkin) to turn down his too-loud music. Rather than obey, however, McCauley aims enormous amplifiers at his father, hits one incredibly loud power-chord on his guitar and sends pop flying through the roof of the house. McCauley's mom, played by Peggy Lipton, tells her son that his father will likely be very upset with him "when he comes down."

The video then continues with scenes of Michael dancing with different nationalities of people all over the world (and it is a catchy song), including scenes in a desert and on the Statue of Liberty. Following the dance sequences, the video then shows close-ups of all different nationalities of people singing to Michael's song and transforming into someone else. So far, all well and good.

Then it gets weird.

After the song ends, a black panther is seen on a dark, rainy street at night. The panther morphs into Michael Jackson, who then explodes in a tantrum of rage and violence—smashing a window with a garbage can, beating the hell out of a car with a tire iron, madly screaming into the night sky—before he transforms back into the panther and vanishes into the night.

This coda to the video was so upsetting to so many people (at one point Michael lecherously grabs his own crotch) that the ending was eliminated from the video and the version shown today has no morphing panther. Yes, that's right: If you missed the first showing of the video, you missed your chance to see it as it was originally produced. Due to the controversy surrounding it, the unexpurgated *Black or White* only ran in its entirety once.

MORRIS THE 9 LIVES CAT

"People make great companions for cats because they practically take care of themselves...all a cat has to do is purr and rub against their legs every now and then and they're content."

—Morris

Morris is another "commercial cat" who became so popular he moved out of the narrow universe of ads and became a cult figure in his own right. Morris the First was born in 1968 and was discovered by 9Lives Cat Food at the Hinsdale, Illinois Humane Society in a suburb of Chicago. He made his TV commercial debut a year later. Morris the First visited the White House, signed (pawed) a Bill, appeared in movies (*Shamus*, with Burt Reynolds, for one), and graced the covers of many national magazines. Morris the first died in 1978 and is buried in Chicago, Illinois at the home of his trainer, the late Lee Duncan. Since Morris the First's death, other felines have inherited his world-renowned mantle as the most recognizable cat in the world. One of the more recent Morrises is an author and has written three books, *The Morris Approach* (1980), dealing with cat care issues; *The Morris Method* (1980), a guide for new pet owners that's been distributed in adoption kits; and *The Morris Prescription* (1986), focused on improving feline healthcare. Also, Morris ran for United States president in 1988 and 1992 on the Finicky Party platform. (Voting records from the period are somewhat unclear as to how many votes Morris actually received. Perhaps we need a recount? Anyone in Florida interested?)

THE "MTM PRODUCTIONS" KITTEN

The meowing kitten logo of MTM Productions closed several legendary TV shows from the 70s, including *The Mary Tyler Moore Show*, *Rhoda*, and *Lou Grant*. These were what you might describe as the "MTM Kitten Classic" shows. In the 1980s, the production company began having some fun with their kitty, and began using a slightly modified version for the closing credits of *Hill Street Blues*, *St. Elsewhere*, and *Newhart*. At the end of Hill Street Blues, the kitten was seen wearing a police cap. At the end of St. Elsewhere, the kitten was dressed in doctor's surgical green scrubs. At the end of Newhart, the kitten was silenced and its "meow" was replaced by the voice of Bob Newhart himself saying, "Meow."

MUFASA, SIMBA, AND NALA FROM "THE LION KING"

These three felines are the main characters in Disney's enormously popular 1994 animated movie *The Lion King*. When you consider the *Lion King* action figures, and *Lion King* toys, and *Lion King* books, and *Lion King* CDs, Mufasa, Simba, and Nala may turn out to be the most seen, known, and recognizable animals in all of pop culture and cinematic history.

The movie tells the story of a Simba, a lion cub who is raised to take the place of his father Mufasa, the King of the jungle. Simba's ascension to power is thwarted, however, by his uncle Scar, an evil lion with a black mane. Simba ultimately usurps Scar, reclaims his rightful place in the "circle of life" as King of the jungle and marries his Queen, Nala.

The Lion King was followed by a straight-to-video sequel (*The Lion King: Simba's Pride*), a Broadway musical, and an animated TV series (not to mention the aforementioned Lion King merchandise).

NASTASSJA KINSKI AND MALCOLM MACDOWELL WHEN THEY TRANSFORM INTO PANTHERS IN "CAT PEOPLE"

There are definite reasons why the 1982 thriller *Cat People* has maintained a cult following these many years. The tagline of the film is "An Erotic Fantasy For The Animal In Us All" and they're not kidding about the "erotic" part. The dark sensuality and incredible panther transformation scenes are a big part of the continuing popularity of this film over the years and why the movie continues to fascinate now on video and DVD. The cats in this movie are gorgeous (Kinski ain't bad, either) and director Paul Schrader takes the premise of the 1942 Val Lewton film of the same name and remakes it with an emphasis on violence and nudity, elements that could only be hinted at in the original. The idea that there is a race of humans that transform into supernatural cat creatures when they have sex and cannot get back to being human unless they kill, is mythical and weird, but ultimately a little silly. Nonetheless, *Cat People* acknowledges the mythic vibe that emanates from cats (let's face it, a similarly-themed movie called Dog People would be ridiculous) and the film is well worth checking out if you're a cat lover and don't mind some gratuitous limb amputations, frequent nudity, and interspecies incest.

OTIS THE CAT IN "THE ADVENTURES OF MILO AND OTIS"

The story of Otis the cat and his pal Milo the dog, two animal friends who wander away from their farm and have all kinds of adventures and get into all manner of predicaments, was told in a 1989 film that was charmingly narrated by Dudley Moore. Otis was "born" and his story was originally told in Japan in 1986 (the film was directed by Japanese director Masanori Hata) but it was not released in the United States until 1989.

PLUTO THE CAT IN EDGAR ALLAN POE'S STORY, "THE BLACK CAT"

"The Black Cat" was originally published in the *Saturday Evening Post* in August 1843 and it is one of Poe's most popular—and chilling—short stories.

Pluto, the black cat of the title, was "remarkably large...beautiful...entirely black, and sagacious to an astonishing degree." The narrator of the tale is, ostensibly, an animal lover, but begins brutalizing his wife and Pluto after sinking into the depths of alcoholism. One night, when Pluto attacks him in self-defense, the narrator gouges out one of the cat's eyes and then hangs him in the garden. Later that same evening, his house burns down, destroying everything, and leaving him destitute. Upon returning to the scene of the fire, the narrator sees that one wall of the house had not burnt, and on it, to his horror, was an image of a cat with a rope around its neck. He ultimately dismisses this as nothing but a ghostly burn from the heat of the fire consuming the cat's corpse and leaving a residue, but he remains haunted by the

Edgar Allan Poe.

sight. The narrator later finds a black cat with one eye who follows him home. Is this Pluto? No, because this new cat has a white patch of fur and Pluto was all black. But why does this cat appear after the tragic sequence of events the narrator has recently endured and what effect will this cat have on the narrator's fate? Poe builds the tension with solemn gravity until the dramatic end, in which Pluto ultimately exacts his revenge on his previous owner.

Such a summary cannot do justice to this terrific short story and thus, here is Edgar Allan Poe's "The Black Cat," reprinted in its entirety as it was originally published in 1843.

🐈 🐈 🐈

"THE BLACK CAT" BY EDGAR ALLAN POE

For the most wild, yet most homely narrative which I am about to pen, I neither expect nor solicit belief. Mad indeed would I be to expect it, in a case where my very senses reject their own evidence. Yet, mad am I not—and very surely do I not dream. But to-morrow I die, and to-day I would unburthen my soul. My immediate purpose is to place before the world, plainly, succinctly, and without comment, a series of mere household events. In their consequences, these events have terrified—have tortured—have destroyed me. Yet I will not attempt to expound them. To me, they have presented little but Horror—to many they will seem less terrible than barroques. Hereafter, perhaps, some intellect may be found which will reduce my phantasm to the common-place—some intellect more calm, more logical, and far less excitable than my own, which will perceive, in the circumstances I detail with awe, nothing more than an ordinary succession of very natural causes and effects.

From my infancy I was noted for the docility and humanity of my disposition. My tenderness of heart was even so conspicuous as to make me the jest of my companions. I was especially fond of animals, and was indulged by my parents with a great variety of pets. With these I spent most of my time, and never was so happy as when feeding and caressing them. This peculiarity of character grew with my growth, and in my manhood, I derived from it one of my principal sources of pleasure. To those who have cherished an affection for a faithful and sagacious dog,

I need hardly be at the trouble of explaining the nature or the intensity of the gratification thus derivable. There is something in the unselfish and self-sacrificing love of a brute, which goes directly to the heart of him who has had frequent occasion to test the paltry friendship and gossamer fidelity of mere *Man*.

I married early, and was happy to find in my wife a disposition not uncongenial with my own. Observing my partiality for domestic pets, she lost no opportunity of procuring those of the most agreeable kind. We had birds, goldfish, a fine dog, rabbits, a small monkey, and *a cat*.

This latter was a remarkably large and beautiful animal, entirely black, and sagacious to an astonishing degree. In speaking of his intelligence, my wife, who at heart was not a little tinctured with superstition, made frequent allusion to the ancient popular notion, which regarded all black cats as witches in disguise. Not that she was ever *serious* upon this point—and I mention the matter at all for no better reason than that it happens, just now, to be remembered.

Pluto—this was the cat's name—was my favorite pet and playmate. I alone fed him, and he attended me wherever I went about the house. It was even with difficulty that I could prevent him from following me through the streets.

Our friendship lasted, in this manner, for several years, during which my general temperament and character—through the instrumentality of the Fiend Intemperance—had (I blush to confess it) experienced a radical alteration for the worse.

I grew, day by day, more moody, more irritable, more regardless of the feelings of others. I suffered myself to use intemperate language to my wife. At length, I even offered her personal violence. My pets, of course, were made to feel the change in my disposition. I not only neglected, but ill-used them. For Pluto, however, I still retained sufficient regard to restrain me from maltreating him, as I made no scruple of maltreating the rabbits, the monkey, or even the dog, when by accident, or through affection, they came in my way. But my disease grew upon me—for what disease is like Alcohol!—and at length even Pluto, who was now becoming old, and consequently somewhat peevish—even Pluto began to experience the effects of my ill temper.

One night, returning home, much intoxicated, from one of my haunts about town, I fancied that the cat avoided my presence. I seized him; when, in his fright at my violence, he inflicted a slight wound upon my hand with his teeth. The fury of a demon instantly possessed me. I knew myself no longer. My original soul seemed, at once, to take its flight from my body and a more than fiendish malevolence, gin-nurtured, thrilled every fibre of my frame. I took from my waistcoat-pocket a pen-knife, opened it, grasped the poor beast by the throat, and deliberately cut one of its eyes from the socket! I blush, I burn, I shudder, while I pen the damnable atrocity.

When reason returned with the morning—when I had slept off the fumes of the night's debauch—I experienced a sentiment half of horror, half of remorse, for the crime of which I had been guilty; but it was, at best, a feeble and equivocal feeling, and the soul remained untouched. I again plunged into excess, and soon drowned in wine all memory of the deed.

In the meantime the cat slowly recovered. The socket of the lost eye presented, it is true, a frightful appearance, but he no longer appeared to suffer any pain. He went about the house as usual, but, as might be expected, fled in extreme terror at my approach. I had so much of my old heart left, as to be at first grieved by this evident dislike on the part of a creature which had once so loved me. But this feeling soon gave place to irritation. And then came, as if to my final and irrevocable overthrow, the spirit of PERVERSENESS. Of this spirit philosophy takes no account. Yet I am not more sure that my soul lives, than I am that perverseness is one of the primitive impulses of the human heart—one of the indivisible primary faculties, or sentiments, which give direction to the character of Man. Who has not, a hundred times, found himself committing a vile or a silly action, for no other reason than because he knows he should not? Have we not a perpetual inclination, in the teeth of our best judgment, to violate that which is *Law*, merely because we understand it to be such? This spirit of perverseness, I say, came to my final overthrow. It was this unfathomable longing of the soul *to vex itself*—to offer violence to its own nature—to do wrong for the wrong's sake only—that urged me to continue and finally to consummate the injury I had inflicted upon the unoffending brute. One morning, in cool blood, I slipped a noose about its neck and hung it to the limb of a tree;—hung it with the tears streaming from my eyes, and with the bitterest remorse at my heart;—hung it *because* I knew that it had loved me, and *because* I felt it had given me no reason of offence;—hung it *because* I knew that in so doing I was committing a sin—a deadly sin that would so jeopardize my immortal soul as to place it—if such a thing wore possible—even beyond the reach of the infinite mercy of the Most Merciful and Most Terrible God.

On the night of the day on which this cruel deed was done, I was aroused from sleep by the cry of fire. The curtains of my bed were in flames. The whole house was blazing. It was with great difficulty that my wife, a servant, and myself, made our escape from the conflagration. The destruction was complete. My entire worldly wealth was swallowed up, and I resigned myself thenceforward to despair.

I am above the weakness of seeking to establish a sequence of cause and effect, between the disaster and the atrocity. But I am detailing a chain of facts—and wish not to leave even a possible link imperfect. On the day succeeding the fire, I visited the ruins. The walls, with one exception, had fallen in. This exception was found in a compartment wall, not very thick, which stood about the middle of the house, and against which had rested the head of my bed. The plastering had here, in great measure, resisted the action of the fire—a fact which I attributed to its having been recently spread. About this wall a dense crowd were collected, and many persons seemed to be examining a particular portion of it with very minute and eager attention. The words "strange!" "singular!" and other similar expressions, excited my curiosity. I approached and saw, as if graven *in bas relief* upon the white surface, the figure of a gigantic *cat*. The impression was given with an accuracy truly marvellous. There was a rope about the animal's neck.

When I first beheld this apparition—for I could scarcely regard it as less—my wonder and my terror were extreme. But at length reflection came to my aid. The cat, I remembered, had been hung in a garden adjacent to the house. Upon the alarm of fire, this garden had been immediately filled by the crowd—by some one of whom the animal must have been cut from the tree and thrown, through an open window, into my chamber. This had probably been done with the view of arousing me from sleep. The falling of other walls had compressed the victim of my cruelty into the substance of the freshly-spread plaster; the lime of which, with the flames, and the *ammonia* from the carcass, had then accomplished the portraiture as I saw it.

Although I thus readily accounted to my reason, if not altogether to my conscience, for the startling fact just detailed, it did not the less fail to make a deep impression upon my fancy. For months I could not rid myself of the phantasm of the cat; and, during this period, there came back into my spirit a half-sentiment that seemed, but was not, remorse. I went so far as to regret the loss of the animal, and to look about me, among the vile haunts which I now habitually frequented, for another pet of the same species, and of somewhat similar appearance, with which to supply its place.

One night as I sat, half stupefied, in a den of more than infamy, my attention was suddenly drawn to some black object, reposing upon the head of one of the immense hogsheads of Gin, or of Rum, which constituted the chief furniture of the apartment. I had been looking steadily at the top of this hogshead for some minutes, and what now caused me surprise was the fact that I had not sooner perceived the object thereupon. I approached it, and touched it with my hand. It was a black cat—a very large one—fully as large as Pluto, and closely resembling him in every respect but one. Pluto had not a white hair upon any portion of his body; but this cat had a large, although indefinite splotch of white, covering nearly the whole region of the breast. Upon my touching him, he immediately arose, purred loudly, rubbed against my hand, and appeared delighted with my notice. This, then, was the very creature of which I was in search. I at once offered to purchase it of the landlord; but this person made no claim to it—knew nothing of it—had never seen it before.

I continued my caresses, and, when I prepared to go home, the animal evinced a disposition to accompany me. I permitted it to do so; occasionally stooping and patting it as I proceeded. When it reached the house it domesticated itself at once, and became immediately a great favorite with my wife.

For my own part, I soon found a dislike to it arising within me. This was just the reverse of what I had anticipated; but—I know not how or why it was—its evident fondness for myself rather disgusted and annoyed. By slow degrees, these feelings of disgust and annoyance rose into the bitterness of hatred. I avoided the creature; a certain sense of shame, and the remembrance of my former deed of cruelty, preventing me from physically abusing it. I did not, for some weeks, strike, or otherwise violently ill use it; but gradually—very gradually—I came to look upon it with unutterable loathing, and to flee silently from its odious presence, as from the breath of a pestilence.

What added, no doubt, to my hatred of the beast, was the discovery, on the morning after I brought it home, that, like Pluto, it also had been deprived of one of its eyes. This circumstance, however, only endeared it to my wife, who, as I have already said, possessed, in a high degree, that humanity of feeling which had once been my distinguishing trait, and the source of many of my simplest and purest pleasures.

With my aversion to this cat, however, its partiality for myself seemed to increase. It followed my footsteps with a pertinacity which it would be difficult to make the reader comprehend. Whenever I sat, it would crouch beneath my chair, or spring upon my knees, covering me with its loathsome caresses. If I arose to walk it would get between my feet and thus nearly throw me down, or, fastening its long and sharp claws in my dress, clamber, in this manner, to my breast. At such times, although I longed to destroy it with a blow, I was yet withheld from so doing, partly by a memory of my former crime, but chiefly—let me confess it at once—by absolute dread of the beast.

This dread was not exactly a dread of physical evil—and yet I should be at a loss how otherwise to define it. I am almost ashamed to own—yes, even in this felon's cell, I am almost ashamed to own - that the terror and horror with which the animal inspired me, had been heightened by one of the merest chimaeras it would be possible to conceive. My wife had called my attention, more than once, to the character of the mark of white hair, of which I have spoken, and which constituted the sole visible difference between the strange beast and the one I had destroyed. The reader will remember that this mark, although large, had been originally very indefinite; but, by slow degrees—degrees nearly imperceptible, and which for a long time my Reason struggled to reject as fanciful—it had, at length, assumed a rigorous distinctness of outline. It was now the representation of an object that I shudder to name—and for this, above all, I loathed, and dreaded, and would have rid myself of the monster *had I dared*—it was now, I say, the image of a hideous—of a ghastly thing—of the GALLOWS !—oh, mournful and terrible engine of Horror and of Crime—of Agony and of Death !

And now was I indeed wretched beyond the wretchedness of mere Humanity. And *a brute beast* - whose fellow I had contemptuously destroyed—*a brute beast* to work out for *me*—for me a man, fashioned in the image of the High God—so much of insufferable wo! Alas! neither by day nor by night knew I the blessing of Rest any more! During the former the creature left me no moment alone; and, in the latter, I started, hourly, from dreams of unutterable fear, to find the hot breath of *the thing* upon my face, and its vast weight - an incarnate Night-Mare that I had no power to shake off - incumbent eternally upon my *heart!*

Beneath the pressure of torments such as these, the feeble remnant of the good within me succumbed. Evil thoughts became my sole intimates—the darkest and most evil of thoughts. The moodiness of my usual temper increased to hatred of all things and of all mankind; while, from the sudden, frequent, and ungovernable outbursts of a fury to which I now blindly abandoned myself, my uncomplaining wife, alas! was the most usual and the most patient of sufferers.

One day she accompanied me, upon some household errand, into the cellar of the old building which our poverty compelled us to inhabit. The cat followed me down the steep stairs, and, nearly throwing me headlong, exasperated me to madness. Uplifting an axe, and forgetting, in my wrath, the childish dread which had hitherto stayed my hand, I aimed a blow at the animal which, of course, would have proved instantly fatal had it descended as I wished. But this blow was arrested by the hand of my wife. Goaded, by the interference, into a rage more than demoniacal, I withdrew my arm from her grasp and buried the axe in her brain. She fell dead upon the spot, without a groan.

This hideous murder accomplished, I set myself forthwith, and with entire deliberation, to the task of concealing the body. I knew that I could not remove it from the house, either by day or by night, without the risk of being observed by the neighbors. Many projects entered my mind. At one period I thought of cutting the corpse into minute fragments, and destroying them by fire. At another, I resolved to dig a grave for it in the floor of the cellar. Again, I deliberated about casting it in the well in the yard—about packing it in a box, as if merchandize, with the usual arrangements, and so getting a porter to take it from the house. Finally I hit upon what I considered a far better expedient than either of these. I determined to wall it up in the cellar—as the monks of the middle ages are recorded to have walled up their victims.

For a purpose such as this the cellar was well adapted. Its walls were loosely constructed, and had lately been plastered throughout with a rough plaster, which the dampness of the atmosphere had prevented from hardening. Moreover, in one of the walls was a projection, caused by a false chimney, or fireplace, that had been filled up, and made to resemble the red of the cellar. I made no doubt that I could readily displace the bricks at this point, insert the corpse, and wall the whole up as before, so that no eye could detect any thing suspicious. And in this calculation I was not deceived. By means of a crow-bar I easily dislodged the bricks, and, having carefully deposited the body against the inner wall, I propped it in that position, while, with little trouble, I re-laid the whole structure as it originally stood. Having procured mortar, sand, and hair, with every possible precaution, I prepared a plaster which could not be distinguished from the old, and with this I very carefully went over the new brickwork. When I had finished, I felt satisfied that all was right. The wall did not present the slightest appearance of having been disturbed. The rubbish on the floor was picked up with the minutest care. I looked around triumphantly, and said to myself—"Here at least, then, my labor has not been in vain."

My next step was to look for the beast which had been the cause of so much wretchedness; for I had, at length, firmly resolved to put it to death. Had I been able to meet with it, at the moment, there could have been no doubt of its fate; but it appeared that the crafty animal had been alarmed at the violence of my previous anger, and forebore to present itself in my present mood. It is impossible to describe, or to imagine, the deep, the blissful sense of relief which the absence of the detested creature occasioned in my bosom. It did not make its appearance during the night—and thus for one night at least, since its introduction into the house, I soundly and tranquilly slept; aye, slept even with the burden of murder upon my soul!

The second and the third day passed, and still my tormentor came not. Once again I breathed as a free man. The monster, in terror, had fled the premises forever! I should behold it no more! My happiness was supreme! The guilt of my dark deed disturbed me but little. Some few inquiries had been made, but these had been readily answered. Even a search had been instituted—but of course nothing was to be discovered. I looked upon my future felicity as secured.

Upon the fourth day of the assassination, a party of the police came, very unexpectedly, into the house, and proceeded again to make rigorous investigation of the premises. Secure, however, in the inscrutability of my place of concealment, I felt no embarrassment whatever. The officers bade me accompany them in their search. They left no nook or corner unexplored. At length, for the third or fourth time, they descended into the cellar. I quivered not in a muscle. My heart beat calmly as that of one who slumbers in innocence. I walked the cellar from end to end. I folded my arms upon my bosom, and roamed easily to and fro. The police were thoroughly satisfied and prepared to depart. The glee at my heart was too strong to be restrained. I burned to say if but one word, by way of triumph, and to render doubly sure their assurance of my guiltlessness.

"Gentlemen," I said at last, as the party ascended the steps, "I delight to have allayed your suspicions. I wish you all health, and a little more courtesy. By the bye, gentlemen, this—this is a very well constructed house." (In the rabid desire to say something easily, I scarcely knew what I uttered at all.)—"I may say an *excellently* well constructed house. These walls are you going, gentlemen?—these walls are solidly put together;" and here, through the mere phrenzy of bravado, I rapped heavily, with a cane which I held in my hand, upon that very portion of the brick-work behind which stood the corpse of the wife of my bosom.

But may God shield and deliver me from the fangs of the Arch-Fiend ! No sooner had the reverberation of my blows sunk into silence, than I was answered by a voice from within the tomb!—by a cry, at first muffled and broken, like the sobbing of a child, and then quickly swelling into one long, loud, and continuous scream, utterly anomalous and inhuman—a howl—a wailing shriek, half of horror and half of triumph, such as might have arisen only out of hell, conjointly from the throats of the dammed in their agony and of the demons that exult in the damnation.

Of my own thoughts it is folly to speak. Swooning, I staggered to the opposite wall. For one instant the party upon the stairs remained motionless, through extremity of terror and of awe. In the next, a dozen stout arms were toiling at the wall. It fell bodily. The corpse, already greatly decayed and clotted with gore, stood erect before the eyes of the spectators. Upon its head, with red extended mouth and solitary eye of fire, sat the hideous beast whose craft had seduced me into murder, and whose informing voice had consigned me to the hangman. I had walled the monster up within the tomb!

PUSS THE CAT IN "PUSS IN BOOTS"

In this classic Mother Goose tale (retold from the original French story "Le Maître Chat ou le chat botté") Puss the cat tricks an ogre into changing himself into a mouse, which he then eats for lunch. This allows Puss's Master to claim the ogre's riches and win the love of a beautiful Princess. For his noble efforts on behalf of his Master, Puss was "promoted" to the position of Lord. Here is the complete text of this beloved story.

THE MASTER CAT; OR, PUSS IN BOOTS

There was a miller who left no more estate to the three sons he had than his mill, his ass, and his cat. The partition was soon made. Neither scrivener nor attorney was sent for. They would soon have eaten up all the poor patrimony. The eldest had the mill, the second the ass, and the youngest nothing but the cat. The poor young fellow was quite comfortless at having so poor a lot.

"My brothers," said he, "may get their living handsomely enough by joining their stocks together; but for my part, when I have eaten up my cat, and made me a muff of his skin, I must die of hunger."

The Cat, who heard all this, but made as if he did not, said to him with a grave and serious air:

"Do not thus afflict yourself, my good master. You have nothing else to do but to give me a bag and get a pair of boots made for me that I may scamper through the dirt and the brambles, and you shall see that you have not so bad a portion in me as you imagine."

The Cat's master did not build very much upon what he said. He had often seen him play a great many cunning tricks to catch rats and mice, as when he used to hang by the heels, or hide himself in the meal, and make as if he were dead; so that he did not altogether despair of his affording him some help in his miserable condition. When the Cat had what he asked for, he booted himself very gallantly, and putting his bag about his neck, he held the strings of it in his two forepaws and went into a warren where there was great abundance of rabbits. He put bran and sow-thistle into his bag, and stretching out at length, as if he had been dead, he waited for some young rabbits, not yet acquainted with the deceits of the world, to come and rummage his bag for what he had put into it.

Scarce was he lain down but he had what he wanted. A rash and foolish young rabbit jumped into his bag, and Monsieur Puss, immediately drawing close the strings, took and killed him without pity. Proud of his prey, he went with it to the palace and asked to speak with his majesty. He was shown upstairs into the King's apartment, and, making a low reverence, said to him:

"I have brought you, sir, a rabbit of the warren, which my noble lord the Marquis of Carabas" (for that was the title which puss was pleased to give his master) "has commanded me to present to your majesty from him."

"Tell thy master," said the king, "that I thank him and that he does me a great deal of pleasure."

Another time he went and hid himself among some standing corn, holding still his bag open, and when a brace of partridges ran into it he drew the strings and so caught them both. He went and made a present of these to the king, as he had done before of the rabbit which he took in the warren. The king, in like manner, received the partridges with great pleasure, and ordered him some money for drink.

The Cat continued for two or three months thus to carry his Majesty, from time to time, game of his master's taking. One day in particular, when he knew for certain that he was to take the air along the river-side, with his daughter, the most beautiful princess in the world, he said to his master:

"If you will follow my advice your fortune is made. You have nothing else to do but go and wash yourself in the river, in that part I shall show you, and leave the rest to me."

The Marquis of Carabas did what the Cat advised him to, without knowing why or wherefore. While he was washing, the King passed by, and the Cat began to cry out:

"Help! help! My Lord Marquis of Carabas is going to be drowned."

At this noise the King put his head out of the coach- window, and, finding it was the Cat who had so often brought him such good game, he commanded his guards to run immediately to the assistance of his Lordship the Marquis of Carabas. While they were drawing the poor Marquis out of the river, the Cat came up to the coach and told the King that, while his master was washing, there came by some rogues, who went off with his clothes, though he had cried out: "Thieves! thieves!" several times, as loud as he could.

This cunning Cat had hidden them under a great stone. The King immediately commanded the officers of his wardrobe to run and fetch one of his best suits for the Lord Marquis of Carabas.

The King caressed him after a very extraordinary manner, and as the fine clothes he had given him extremely set off his good mien (for he was well made and very handsome in his person), the King's daughter took a secret inclination to him, and the Marquis of Carabas had no sooner cast two or three respectful and somewhat tender glances but she fell in love with him to distraction. The King would needs have him come into the coach and take part of the airing. The Cat, quite overjoyed to see his project begin to succeed, marched on before, and, meeting with some countrymen, who were mowing a meadow, he said to them:

"Good people, you who are mowing, if you do not tell the King that the meadow you mow belongs to my Lord Marquis of Carabas, you shall be chopped as small as herbs for the pot."

The King did not fail asking of the mowers to whom the meadow they were mowing belonged.

"To my Lord Marquis of Carabas," answered they altogether, for the Cat's threats had made them terribly afraid.

"You see, sir," said the Marquis, "this is a meadow which never fails to yield a plentiful harvest every year."

The Master Cat, who went still on before, met with some reapers, and said to them:

"Good people, you who are reaping, if you do not tell the King that all this corn belongs to the Marquis of Carabas, you shall be chopped as small as herbs for the pot."

The King, who passed by a moment after, would needs know to whom all that corn, which he then saw, did belong.

"To my Lord Marquis of Carabas," replied the reapers, and the King was very well pleased with it, as well as the Marquis, whom he congratulated thereupon. The Master Cat, who went always before, said the same words to all he met, and the King was astonished at the vast estates of my Lord Marquis of Carabas.

Monsieur Puss came at last to a stately castle, the master of which was an ogre, the richest had ever been known; for all the lands which the King had then gone over belonged to this castle. The Cat, who had taken care to inform himself who this ogre was and what he could do, asked to speak with him, saying he could not pass so near his castle without having the honor of paying his respects to him.

The ogre received him as civilly as an ogre could do, and made him sit down.

"I have been assured," said the Cat, "that you have the gift of being able to change yourself into all sorts of creatures you have a mind to; you can, for example, transform yourself into a lion, or elephant, and the like."

"That is true," answered the ogre very briskly; "and to convince you, you shall see me now become a lion."

Puss was so sadly terrified at the sight of a lion so near him that he immediately got into the gutter, not without abundance of trouble and danger, because of his boots, which were of no use at all to him in walking upon the tiles. A little while after, when Puss saw that the ogre had resumed his natural form, he came down, and owned he had been very much frightened.

"I have been, moreover, informed," said the Cat, "but I know not how to believe it, that you have also the power to take on you the shape of the smallest animals; for example, to change yourself into a rat or a mouse; but I must own to you I take this to be impossible."

"Impossible!" cried the ogre; "you shall see that presently."

And at the same time he changed himself into a mouse, and began to run about the floor. Puss no sooner perceived this but he fell upon him and ate him up.

Meanwhile the King, who saw, as he passed, this fine castle of the ogre's, had a mind to go into it. Puss, who heard the noise of his Majesty's coach running over the draw-bridge, ran out, and said to the King:

"Your Majesty is welcome to this castle of my Lord Marquis of Carabas."

"What! my Lord Marquis," cried the King, "and does this castle also belong to you? There can be nothing finer than this court and all the stately buildings which surround it; let us go into it, if you please."

The Marquis gave his hand to the Princess, and followed the King, who went first. They passed into a spacious hall, where they found a magnificent collation, which the ogre had prepared for his friends, who were that very day to visit him, but dared not to enter, knowing the King was there. His Majesty was perfectly charmed with the good qualities of my Lord Marquis of Carabas, as was his daughter, who had fallen violently in love with him, and, seeing the vast estate he possessed, said to him, after having drunk five or six glasses:

"It will be owing to yourself only, my Lord Marquis, if you are not my son-in-law."

The Marquis, making several low bows, accepted the honor which his Majesty conferred upon him, and forthwith, that very same day, married the Princess.

Puss became a great lord, and never ran after mice any more but only for his diversion.

THE PUSSY-CAT IN EDWARD LEAR'S "THE OWL AND THE PUSSY-CAT"

"The Owl And The Pussy-Cat" is probably the best known of Edward Lear's Nonsense songs, and it was written to cheer up the sick daughter of a friend. Here it is for your enjoyment.

🐾 🐾 🐾

"THE OWL AND THE PUSSY-CAT," BY EDWARD LEAR

The Owl and the Pussy-Cat went to sea
In a beautiful pea-green boat:
They took some honey, and plenty of money
Wrapped up in a five-pound note.
The Owl looked up to the stars above,
And sang to a small guitar,
"O lovely Pussy, O Pussy, my love,
What a beautiful Pussy you are,
You are,
You are!
What a beautiful Pussy you are!"
Pussy said to the Owl, "You elegant fowl,

How charmingly sweet you sing!

Oh! let us be married; too long we have tarried:

But what shall we do for a ring?"

They sailed away, for a year and a day,

To the land where the bong-tree grows;

And there in a wood a Piggy-wig stood,

With a ring at the end of his nose,

His nose,

His nose,

With a ring at the end of his nose.

"Dear Pig, are you willing to sell for one shilling

Your ring?" Said the Piggy, "I will."

So they took it away, and were married next day

By the Turkey who lives on the hill.

They dined on mince and slices of quince,

Which they ate with a runcible spoon;

And hand in hand on the edge of the sand

They danced by the light of the moon,

The moon,

The moon,

They danced by the light of the moon.

THE PUSSYCATS FROM "JOSIE AND THE PUSSYCATS"

The 2001 live-action movie *Josie and the Pussycats* was based on the all-girl-band of the same name from the *Archie* comics and starred Rachel Leigh Cook (as Josie), Tara Reid, and Rachel Dawson as the Pussycats. *Josie and the Pussycats* was also an animated series on TV from 1970 to 1972; followed by a spin-off, *Josie and the Pussycats in Outer Space*, from 1972-1974.

SCHRÖDINGER'S CAT

Physicist Erwin Schrödinger's cat is probably the most famous and influential cat in science—and yet he wasn't even real! (And I say that without the least sense of irony.) Schrödinger postulated a "thought experiment" in which a cat is placed in a locked room with a sealed flask of prussic acid, over which was suspended a hammer on a string. The string will release the hammer and break the flask if any radioactivity is registered on a Geiger counter in the next room. Sitting next to the Geiger counter is a quantity of radioactive material that has exactly a 50 percent chance of releasing radioactivity within an hour. Schrödinger theorized that, since the fate of the cat was linked to the release of the radioactivity, and until someone came to observe the result, the room must contain a wave-form of a half-dead, half-live cat. This was supposed to illustrate the quantum physics theory called superposition, which suggests that at the subatomic level, the same atom can co-exist in two separate realities at the same time (as does Schrödinger's cat). Personally, I feel sorry for the cat, whose fate supposedly hinges on whether or not someone actually looks inside the room to see if the acid has killed him or not. The looking apparently affects the results. Until someone bothers to check, the cat is half dead and half alive. Reminds you of Church in *Pet Sematary*, doesn't it?

SALEM SABERHAGEN FROM "SABRINA THE TEENAGE WITCH"

Salem Saberhagen is really a warlock who has been sentenced by the Witches Council to live as a cat (with no magical powers) for 100 years because of his failed attempt to take over the world. (Can't say he wasn't ambitious, eh?) In the first season of *Sabrina the Teenage Witch*, Salem was approximately 25 years old, with another 75 years to go in his "sentence." Salem is an American Shorthair and his favorite magazine is *The Economist*. At one point Salem had a girlfriend named Shelly, played by model/actress Kathy Ireland but that relationship is now over since she is a woman and Salem is a cat. Salem has won many "Favorite Animal" awards and has a very pleasing singing voice.

SASSY, THE HOMEWARD BOUND CAT

Sally Field voiced this loveable kitty in the successful *Homeward Bound* movies, the first of which (*Homeward Bound: The Incredible Journey*, 1994) was a remake of Disney's equally popular 1963 classic, *The Incredible Journey*. The 1994 movie was followed in 1996 by a sequel, *Homeward Bound II: Lost in San Francisco*.

SCRATCHY THE CAT FROM "THE ITCHY AND SCRATCHY SHOW" SEEN ON "THE SIMPSONS"

Scratchy the cat is the repeat target of Itchy the mouse on the show bearing their name, which is seen as a "show within a show" on the series *The Simpsons*, and which can be viewed as a warped version of the *Tom and Jerry* cartoons. Scratchy has been through the ringer, literally (much to the delight of Bart Simpson). Some of the torments and abuses he has endured at the paws of Itchy have included:

(**Note:** Spoilers and extreme grossness follow)

- having a flaming arrow shot into his rear.
- being beheaded in a guillotine and then having his severed head blown up by a firecracker.
- being stabbed in the heart with a butcher knife.
- having his head blown off by a bazooka and then blowing up his own head when he unwittingly inserts cherry bombs into his empty eye sockets.
- having his body liquefied in a blender.
- eating a meatball bomb.
- drinking acid.
- being dismembered by a grain combine.
- having a nail hammered into his head followed by a picture being hung on the nail.
- being eaten by an alligator.
- having his tongue tied to a rocket headed for the moon.
- having his tongue caught in the automatic ball return at a bowling alley and then being dismembered (his body parts sold to dogs) by a bowling ball bomb.
- having his heart ripped out as a Valentine's Day present.
- having his head covered with flesh-eating ants.
- having his feet nailed to the stairs of an escalator and then being eaten by the machine.
- having his internal organs ripped out when his tonsils are tied to a brick and the brick is thrown out a window.
- being sliced to bits by a spaying laser.

SOCKS, THE (FORMER) FIRST CAT

In 1992, Socks the cat was plucked out of his halcyon existence in Arkansas and transplanted to Washington, D.C., where he suddenly had to, first, deal with the White House Press Corps, and then, in a development of unthinkable implications, a dog. President Clinton's dog Buddy and Socks the cat did not get along. They did manage to live together more or less peacefully under the same Presidential roof while Bill Clinton was in office, but Socks did not make the trip to Chappaqua, New York with the Clintons when they vacated the White House in 2001. To everyone's surprise, Socks was adopted by Clinton's secretary Betty Currie. In all likelihood, he is probably enjoying life more now out of the spotlight (and away from the annoying Buddy). Socks had his own fan club and there were countless Web sites devoted to him, and even two books published about Socks: *Children's Letters to Socks* (Birch Lane Press, 1994); *Dear Socks, Dear Buddy: Kids' Letters to the First Pets* (Intro by Hillary) Simon and Schuster, 1998)

THE SPHINX

The Sphinx is a mythical creature with the body of a lion and the head of a man.

SPHINX FACTS

(Try saying *that* five times fast!)

- The Great Sphinx at Giza has been stoically staring out over the Egyptian desert for 4,500 years. (It is believed to have been built aroud 2500 B.C.)
- The body of the Sphinx is 250 feet long and 65 feet tall.)
- The paws of the Sphinx are 50 feet long.
- The face of the Sphinx is 13 feet wide.
- The eyes of the Sphinx are 6 feet high
- The beard from the Sphinx is on display in the British Museum
- The Sphinx is built from sandstone, which is very soft. The only reason it has survived this long is because it was completely buried

many times for thousands of years, and, thus, protected from wind, rain, sun, and pollution.

- The image of the Sphinx now symbolizes wisdom and power, and is perceived to have been built as a sign of royal authority.

- The latest theory regarding the building of the Sphinx is that it was commissioned by 4th Dynasty King, Khafre, who ruled Egypt from 2558 to 2532 B.C.

- There is a possibility that the Sphinx was originally painted in bright colors.

- Contrary to rumor, the Sphinx's nose was not shot off by Napoleon's men. The Sphinx's nose is broken off because Turks used it for target practice during the time of the Ottoman Empire between the 14th and 20th centuries.

GEO. L. SCHUMAN AND COMPANY

The Great Sphinx at Giza.

- The word "Sphinx" means "strangler." The Greeks first used it to describe a mythical creature that had the body of a lion, the head of a woman, and the wings of a bird. In the story of Oedipus, the Sphinx stopped travelers on the roads to Thebes, and would kill any who could not answer this now-famous riddle: "What creature walks on four legs in the morning, on two legs at noon, and on three legs in the evening?" Oedipus finally came up with the correct answer: human beings, who crawl on all fours as infants, walk upright in maturity, and in old age rely on the "third leg" of a cane.

- In 1988, the left shoulder of the Sphinx fell off. Repair efforts are still underway.

- The face of the Sphinx is thought to be that of Egyptian ruler Chepren, who had his workers build the monumental figure to guard his pyramid tomb (which sits to the north of the Sphinx).

- A recent search of the music Web site CDNow.com found 32 individual songs titled "Sphinx," plus songs called "Dancing Sphinx," "Jiggle of the Sphinx," "Robot Sphinx," "Secrets of the Sphinx," "Sphinx Lightning," "Sphinx Returns," and "The Sphinx Stinks."

SYLVESTER THE CAT FROM THE WARNER BROS. CARTOONS

Are we men, or are we mice?

—Sylvester

Sylvester was the lisping, ravenous Warner Bros. "puddy tat" Tweety Bird always thought he saw (Remember? "I tawt I taw a puddy tat." That was Sylvester!) Hector the dog was another nemesis of Sylvester's.

SYLVIA THE GIANT BLACK CAT IN THE "STAR TREK" EPISODE, "CATSPAW"

"Catspaw" is a first season "Trek Classic" episode. It is episode #30 of the original incarnation of the series and it aired for the first time on October 27, 1967, during Halloween week. "Catspaw" featured Antoinette Bower as Sylvia the supernatural alien witch/shape-changer. On planet Pyris VII, Kirk and company come upon what appears to be an undeniably Earthlike haunted castle in which they find crew members Sulu and Scotty, in some kind of zombielike state. Bent on conquest, two aliens named Korob and Sylvia have utilized a transmuting device to look human and they try to exploit human fears to overwhelm and overcome the Enterprise crew. Korob and Sylvia (in the guise of a witch and a warlock) do everything in their power to terrify Kirk and his away team, but their scare tactics have no effect at all on the always logical and utterly emotionless Mr. Spock. Korob ultimately betrays Sylvia and that is when she transforms into a giant black cat and destroys her one-time ally. Eventually Kirk is able to destroy the "magic wand" type device that has been duping them into a false perception of their surroundings and the aliens are revealed for what they truly are: weird little creatures who are not the least bit frightening when seen in their natural form. Live long and prosper.

THOMASINA THE CAT FROM "THE THREE LIVES OF THOMASINA"

The movie *The Three Lives of Thomasina* (1974), was based on the acclaimed novel *Thomasina* by Paul Gallico and it told the story of Mary's injured cat, Thomasina, who couldn't even be cured by Mary's veterinarian dad. Mary turns for help to a mysterious "witch" who teaches her and Thomasina about the healing power of love.

TOM CAT, THE CAT IN THE "TOM AND JERRY" CARTOONS

Tom wanted to nothing more out of life than to snare (and eat, of course) Jerry the mouse. He was always thwarted, however, and the adventures of these two arch nemeses were chronicled in a series of cartoon shorts in the 1960s. Tom and Jerry were "reanimated" in 1992 in a G-rated feature film called *Tom and Jerry: The Movie*, directed by Phil Roman and starring the voices of Richard Kind and Dana Hill.

TONY THE TIGER

Tony the Tiger debuted in 1952 and is sort of like a feline Popeye the Sailor: He garners his strength from a food product, which, in Tony's case, is Frosted Flakes Cereal. (Popeye's, of course, was spinach. Canned spinach, to boot.)

Tony is a big, burly, barrel-chested tiger with a booming, basso profundo voice which he regularly uses to belt out, "THEY'RE GRRRRRRRREAT!" at the end of every Frosted Flakes commercial. (Tony was voiced by the legendary Thurl Ravenscroft, who also supplied the voice for the Grinch in the 1966 classic animated film, *How the Grinch Stole Christmas*. Ravenscroft voiced a third kitty when he played the Russian cat in the 1970 Disney film, *The Aristocats*.

TOONCES THE CAT ON "SATURDAY NIGHT LIVE"

Toonces, the cat who could drive, was a creation of the *Saturday Night Live* writers and the most entertaining aspect of the "Toonces" skits was the obvious, ahem, "stuffed" nature of Toonces himself. Toonces first appeared in May of 1989 with a skit that starred Steve Martin, Dana Carvey, and Victoria Jackson. Steve Martin was initially said to be one of Toonces' co-owners, but following the premiere skit, Toonces belonged to only Dana Carvey and Victoria Jackson (probably because they were cast members and Steve Martin was only an occasional guest host). Toonces could drive a car...just not very well. Toonces appeared in five episodes from 1989 through 1993, with every episode ending in the same scene of Toonces driving himself and his companions off a cliff:

- May 20, 1989, with Guest Host Steve Martin
- December 2, 1989, with Guest Host John Goodman
- March 24, 1990, with Guest Host Debra Winger
- May 19, 1990, with Guest Host Candace Bergen
- February 13, 1993, with Guest Host Alec Baldwin

TOP CAT

We are the Unscratchables.

—Top Cat

A cat who wears a hat and has a posse! This feline might just be the coolest cat ever to prowl an alley (Hoagy's Alley, in TC's case). Top Cat appeared in both an animated series and a comic strip and the character was actually based on Phil Silvers's character Sgt. Ernie Bilko from the sitcom *You'll Never Get Rich* (aka *The Phil Silvers Show*), which ran on CBS from 1955 to 1959. The animated Hanna-Barbera series *Top Cat* debuted in 1961 (with actor Arnold Stang voicing TC) on ABC and lasted one season. Dell Comics and Gold Key Comics published a *Top Cat* comic book from 1962 through 1973. Top Cat also showed up in cameos in some Yogi Bear cartoons in the 70s.

THE 14 MUSCLES OF A CAT

- Facial Muscles—These allow the cat to make limited facial expressions.
- Jaw Muscles—These incredibly powerful muscles allow the cat to exert tremendous pressure when biting.
- Trapezius—These draw the shoulders up.
- Dorsals—These allow the cat to twist and curl its torso.
- Oblique Abdominals—These are layered strap muscles that support the cat's internal organs.
- Sartorius - These allow the cat to raise its knees and rotate its thighs.
- Gluteal Muscles—These extend the hips.
- Tail Muscles—Yes, even your cat's tail has muscles. The tail is not just a long bony appendage covered in skin. Fine muscles allow your kitty to raise, lower, and curl its tail.
- Gastrocnemius—These extend and point the cat's legs.
- Biceps Femoris—These are the muscles that bend the cat's legs.
- Pectorals—These allow the cat to draw back its shoulders and forelegs.
- Digital Extensor Muscles—These are what the cat uses to extend its claws and toes.
- Triceps—These straighten the elbow and draw back the cat's lower leg.
- Deltoid—These pull the cat's shoulders forward.

THE 19 BONES OF A CAT

- Skull—A cat's skull has 29 bones.
- Vertebrae—These are the bones of the cat's neck and spinal column.
- Scapula—This bone, also known as the shoulder blade, attaches to the spine by tendons and muscles.
- Thoracic spikes—These are the bones attached to the muscles of the thorax, the area between the neck and diaphragm and housing the heart and lungs.
- Pelvis—This is a fused ring of bone consisting of the pubis (the front bone of the pelvis), the ilium (the uppermost pelvic bone), and the ischium (the lowest pelvic bone).
- Hip Joint—This is a flexible ball and socket of bone that comprises the cat's hip.
- Mandible—This is the cat's lower jaw bone and is considerably shorter than the same bone of the cat's much larger ancestors.
- Acoustic meatus—These bones protect the entrance of the cat's ear nerves.
- Clavicle—This is the cat's collarbone and it is held in place only by muscles.
- Metacarpals—These are comparable to the bones of the human palm between the wrist and the fingers; in quadripeds (like cats), they are in the forefoot.
- Phalanges—These are the cat's forepaws, and compare to human fingers.
- Foreleg—These are the bones of the cat's front legs.

- Sternum—This is also known as the breastbone.
- Wrists—These are the flexible bones known as carpals that provide increased agility.
- Ribs—A cat has 13 pairs.
- Costal arch—This arch is made of cartilage and consists of the cat's last ribs.
- Costal cartilage—This is the lower end of the cat's ribs.
- Tarsus—This bone sits between the cat's leg and foot.
- Tail—A cat's tail consists of between 18 and 20 bendable and jointed vertebrae. (See **Chapter 8** to learn the secrets of your cat's tail.)

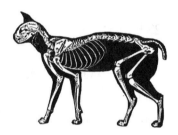

5 DISEASES CAT LOVERS **MUST** VACCINATE THEIR CATS AGAINST

A routine examination each year by a veterinarian is an important part of your cat's health care, and a program of vaccinations should be included to prevent diseases that can kill your cat if he is not protected. Here is a look at five common feline diseases that are almost always preventable if vaccinated against.

1. FELINE LEUKEMIA

Leukemia in cats is caused by the Feline Leukemia Virus (FeLV), which attacks the cat's white blood cells and causes them to multiply at extreme rates and replace normal cells and tissue. This process severely compromises the cat's immune system and allows secondary infections and conditions such as pneumonia, chronic anemia, and lymphosarcoma to run rampant. Signs of Feline Leukemia include loss of appetite or refusal to eat at all, chronic diarrhea and vomiting, weight loss, weakness, fever, difficulty breathing, and coughing. If your cat has not been vaccinated against FeLV and exhibits any of these symptoms, get him to a vet as quickly as possible. Feline Leukemia vaccines should be a routine part of your cat's annual health care. Two initial doses are administered three weeks apart, followed by an annual booster shot.

2. FELINE INFECTIOUS PERITONITIS

Feline Infectious Peritonitis (FIP) is always fatal and is a painful way for a cat to die. Abdominal bloating, caused by an accumulation of fluid, is one of the most prevalent symptoms of FIP. Generalized infection, weight loss, fever, and eye sores are also possible with this disease. Feline Infectious Peritonitis is caused by a virus and the vaccine against it is often administered by inserting drops into the cat's nose. (As you might imagine, cats just love this.) The drops build immunity in the cat's nasal passages which is where the FIP virus usually multiplies and spreads.

3. RABIES

Rabies is caused by a virus spread by the saliva of a rabies-infected animal. It is usually transmitted by a bite. Once the disease progresses, the symptoms include frenzied behavior, dilated pupils, vicious clawing and biting, hoarseness of the throat (from paralysis), and difficulty swallowing. A human can contract rabies if bit by an infected animal, but, again, the saliva of the rabies carrier must enter the bloodstream for a person or another animal to become infected. A scratch from an animal with rabies will not necessarily cause rabies. Rabies is always fatal once the disease progresses to the point of symptoms, but is it reversible if caught within ten days of infection. All cats—even indoor cats—should be vaccinated annually against rabies. Cats who are always kept inside do go outdoors on occasion, such as for vet visits; and there is also the real possibility that a rabies-infected bat or other animal can get into your house and bite your cat. Rabies is a horrible disease and since it can almost always be prevented, there is no excuse for not annually vaccinating against this disease.

4. FELINE PANLEUKOPENIA

Feline Panleukopenia (FPL) is also known as feline distemper and is very common in cats. (Other names for this disease include cat fever, cat plague, and yellow vomit.) FPL is highly contagious from cat to cat, yet the good news is that it is preventable and treatable. The incubation period for FPL is only two to nine days and, thus, early detection in non-vaccinated cats is critical for survival. Symptoms of this disease include vomiting, yellow diarrhea, extreme thirst (cats will often lie with their head over their water dish but not drink), high fever, loss of appetite, matted fur, a film over the eyes, a tender abdomen, and a spread-eagled posture. If not treated early, a cat can die within a week from this disease. The FPL vaccine can be given to kittens between six and 12 weeks of age, followed by an annual booster.

5. FELINE RESPIRATORY DISEASE

Most feline respiratory diseases are caused by one of two viruses, the feline viral rhinoetracheitis (FVR) or the feline calcivirus (FCV). Feline respiratory disease can be spread from cat to cat by sneezes or coughs and can turn into pneumonia, which can be fatal to kittens. The symptoms of Feline Respiratory Disease are red and inflamed eyes, watery or sticky discharge from the nose and eyes, sores in the mouth and nose, and fever. The more serious of these two virus-caused respiratory diseases is rhinoetracheitis, which can cause pregnant cats to spontaneously abort. Cats can be protected against both of these viruses with a single vaccination.

25 STATES WHERE RABIES VACCINATION FOR CATS ARE REQUIRED BY LAW

- Alabama
- Alaska
- Arkansas
- Connecticut
- Delaware
- Florida
- Georgia
- Indiana
- Louisiana
- Maine
- Maryland
- Massachusetts
- Mississippi
- Nebraska
- New Hampshire
- New Mexico
- North Carolina
- Pennsylvania
- Rhode Island
- Tennessee
- Texas
- Vermont
- Virginia
- West Virginia
- Wyoming

Of the remaining 25 states, 13 have some local laws that require rabies vaccinations for cats, and 12 states have no requirement at all for rabies vaccinations.

20 COMMON CAT AILMENTS AND THEIR 14 SYMPTOMS

Many of these conditions are relatively benign and treatable and, thus, nipping feline health problems in the bud is the prudent (and compassionate) thing to do. After all, kitty can't get to the doctor herself, so she needs you to keep track of her overall health.

The first list is a rundown of the 14 most common symptoms associated with cat ailments. If your cat is exhibiting signs of any of these, this chart will allow you to make an educated guess as to what might be the problem.

The second section of this chapter is a breakdown of the 20 most common cat ailments with a list of their symptoms. Your cat will not have all the listed symptoms for each ailment described in the list below, but you need to monitor your pet for any and all of these symptoms on a regular basis.

For example, if your cat is sneezing, you can immediately tell from these charts that it is probably due to allergies or a head cold—but it could be distemper. You can then watch her for changes or an exacerbation of symptoms or even new symptoms and hopefully figure out what's ailing kitty (as best as possible) before you call or visit the vet to discuss treatment. Your vet looks to you to accurately identify and describe your cat's symptoms so he or she can know what to prescribe for treatment.

SYMPTOMS TO WATCH OUT FOR...

1. Breathing difficulties: H, K, N, Q, S
2. Changes in the skin: A, I, T
3. Constipation: B, H, J, L, M, Q, S, T

123

4. Coughing: D, H
5. Diarrhea: J, M, N, P, Q, S, T
6. Fever: D, G, J, O
7. Head shaking: F
8. Increased/excessive thirst: G, M, N, O, P, R
9. Pallor of the mucus membranes: M, N, O, P, Q, R, S, T
10. Scratching the ears: F
11. Sneezing: A,E, K
12. Swelling of the body: E, G, H, N
13. Swollen lymph nodes: C, D, K, N
14. Vomiting: B, C, H, J, K, L, M, N, O, P, Q, R, S

A. ALLERGIES

2. Changes in the skin
4. Coughing
11. Sneezing

B. BLOCKAGE OF THE INTESTINES

3. Constipation
13. Swollen lymph nodes
14. Vomiting

C. DENTAL PROBLEMS

12. Swelling of the body
13. Swollen lymph nodes
14. Vomiting

D. DISEASES/DISORDERS OF THE UPPER RESPIRATORY SYSTEM

1. Breathing difficulties
4. Coughing
6. Fever
12. Swelling of the body

E. DISTEMPER

11. Sneezing

F. EAR INFECTION

7. Head shaking
10. Scratching the ears

G. FLEAS

6. Fever
8. Increased/excessive thirst
11. Sneezing

H. FOREIGN BODIES

1. Breathing difficulties
3. Constipation
4. Coughing
11. Sneezing
13. Swollen lymph nodes
14. Vomiting

I. FUNGUS

2. Changes in the skin

J. HAIR BALLS

3. Constipation
5. Diarrhea
6. Fever
13. Swollen lymph nodes
14. Vomiting

K. HEAD COLD

1. Breathing difficulties
12. Swelling of the body
13. Swollen lymph nodes
14. Vomiting

L. INFECTIOUS PERITONITIS

3. Constipation
13. Swollen lymph nodes
14. Vomiting

M. KIDNEY STONES

3. Constipation
5. Diarrhea
8. Increased/excessive thirst
9. Pallor of the mucus membranes
13. Swollen lymph nodes
14. Vomiting

N. LEUKEMIA

1. Breathing difficulties
5. Diarrhea
8. Increased/excessive thirst
9. Pallor of the mucus membranes
12. Swelling of the body

13. Swollen lymph nodes
14. Vomiting

O. NEPHRITIS

6. Fever
8. Increased/excessive thirst
9. Pallor of the mucus membranes
13. Swollen lymph nodes
14. Vomiting

P. POISONING

5. Diarrhea
8. Increased/excessive thirst
9. Pallor of the mucus membranes
13. Swollen lymph nodes
14. Vomiting

Q. SHOCK

1. Breathing difficulties
3. Constipation
5. Diarrhea
9. Pallor of the mucus membranes
13. Swollen lymph nodes
14. Vomiting

R. UTERINE INFECTION

8. Increased/excessive thirst
9. Pallor of the mucus membranes
13. Swollen lymph nodes
14. Vomiting

S. WORMS

1. Breathing difficulties
3. Constipation

5. Diarrhea

9. Pallor of the mucus membranes

13. Swollen lymph nodes

14. Vomiting

T. WRONG OR BAD DIET

2. Changes in the skin

3. Constipation

5. Diarrhea

9. Pallor of the mucus membranes

14. Vomiting

MEDICAL INSURANCE FOR CATS

Veterinary insurance for pets is advertised as a way to protect "your pet's health, your savings, and your peace of mind." Many families have had to go through the heartbreak of having their injured or ill cat or dog euthanized because they could not afford the treatment the animal needed. Many pet owners are unprepared for a large medical bill (over $1,000 for instance) for their cat or dog, and veterinary insurance can pay 80 percent of these fees, significantly lessening the financial burden.

For costs ranging from around $9 to $16 per month, depending on your geographical location, age and type of pet, and type of coverage plan you select, a pet owner can buy health insurance for their cat or dog.

Coverage includes payment for routine illnesses, diagnostic tests, surgery, hospitalization, X-rays, specialists, cancer treatments, CAT scans, emergency care, and treatment for poisonings.

There are a variety of plans available and a good place to start is online at these two Web sites:

www.health-insurance-for-pets.com, *www.petinsurance.com*

These sites walk you through a free online quote procedure and you can apply and pay online if you choose to buy coverage.

62 FREE INFORMATION SHEETS ABOUT YOUR CAT'S HEALTH FROM THE FELINE ADVISORY BUREAU

The Feline Advisory Bureau (FAB) is a charitable organization in Great Britain whose sole raison d'etre is to improve the health of cats all around the world. They offer free single copies of informative fact sheets on 62 subjects relating to the health of felines.

FROM THEIR WEB SITE:

The UK's Feline Advisory Bureau was set up in 1958 when a few dedicated cat enthusiasts decided that cats needed treatment based on specialist knowledge and that this knowledge should be made available to veterinary surgeons, cat breeders, cattery proprietors and cat owners.

Over the years the FAB has become synonymous with expertise in feline treatment, both in the veterinary field and for its work improving the standards of boarding catteries. The following information sheets have been put together by experts in the field of feline medicine and are updated regularly.

You may print one copy of each information sheet for your own information. You may not sell them on, reproduce them on the Internet, or reprint them in any publication (in any medium) without the express permission of the Feline Advisory Bureau.

Contacing the Feline Advisory Bureau

Feline Advisory Bureau
'Taeselbury', High Street
Tisbury, Wiltshire, SP3 6LD, UK
Tel: +44(0)1747 871872
Fax: +44(0)1747 871873
e-mail: fab@fabcats.org
Web site: *www.fabcats.org*

127

THE TITLES

- Feline flea control
- Feline Immunodeficiency Virus—FIV
- Feline Leukaemia Virus—FeLV
- Feline upper respiratory tract disease - cat 'flu'
- Worming your cat
- Vaccinating your cat
- The overweight cat
- Neutering your cat
- Euthanasia
- Spraying and soiling indoors
- Caring for the elderly cat
- Caring for your kitten
- Moving house with cats
- Introducing your cat to other cats and dogs
- Scratching or clawing in the house
- Ringworm in cats
- Feline Infectious Peritonitis (FIP)
- Chlamydial infection in cats
- Nervous cats and aggressive cats
- Cats—sorting fact from fiction: cats and babies, zoonoses, allergies
- Choosing a good boarding cattery
- Feline Infectious Anaemia—FIA
- Choosing a veterinary surgeon
- Second opinion (included with above paper)
- Hidden dangers of plants
- Fencing the garden to protect your cat
- Starting a boarding cattery
- Setting up a shelter for rescued cats
- Setting up a neutering project for feral cats
- Hyperthyroidism in cats
- Ringworm (dermatophytosis)—information for breeders
- Poisons in the home
- Polycystic Kidney Disease
- Cat flu—information for breeders

- Chronic Nasal Discharge in the cat
- Cardiomyopathy in cats
- Diarrhea in cats
- Liver disease in cats
- Constipation in cats
- Toxoplasmosis in cats and man
- Diabetes mellitus in the cat
- Cystitis and feline lower urinary tract disease
- Disinfectants
- Mouth problems in the cat
- Harvest mite (Trombicula autumnalis) infestation in the cat
- Solar dermatitis and squamous cell carcinoma
- Anaesthesia and analgesia in the cat
- Feeding cats
- Ear problems in cats
- Evolution of the cat
- Medicating cats
- Conjunctivitis in cats
- Coughing cats
- Post-operative care for cats
- Show procedure, preparation and grooming
- The role of the cat show veterinary surgeon
- Stud cats
- What to do if your cat produces a deformed kitten
- Hand-rearing kittens
- Feline acne and stud tail
- Parturition and its problems in the cat
- Reproductive failure and infertility in the cat
- Kidney disease in the cat

THE 5 MOST POPULAR
CAT FOODS

- Friskies
- 9 Lives
- Alpo
- Banquet
- IAMS Diet

(I feed Carter Triumph Cat Food. He is especially fond of the Beef and Salmon, and the Turkey recipes. He's not too thrilled with the new design of their can labels but this does not deter him from devouring what is in the can.)

27 ADDITIVES IN PROCESSED CAT FOODS

These 27 "substances" are what it takes to process cat food and bring it to market. The vast majority of items on this list are used to give the food a stable shelf life and make it palatable, uniform in texture, and safe to eat. Some of these additives, though, are added to cat food to make it more appealing to humans. For instance, we know that the color of a food isn't high on kitty's list of desirable features of a dish of cat food. But color is added to processed cat food so that we humans (who do, after all, take care of kitty's grocery shopping) will not be repulsed when we open a can of cat food.

Consistency of appearance is more important to us than to our cats. A single meal of cat food is equivalent to five mice but we do not make our domestic cats hunt for food in America. And even though our kitties probably wouldn't mind blood, guts, and eviscera in their bowls (they'd probably love it) we wouldn't stand for it. Thus, cat food manufacturers (with our blessing) add processing and formulation aids, sequestrants, solvents, stabilizers, thickeners, surface active agents, surface finishing agents, synergists, and texturizers, among other goodies, all designed to make a can of cat food as unlike five mice as possible. No mouse tails to fuss with, either.

- ✔ Anticaking agents
- ✔ Antimicrobial agents
- ✔ Antioxidants
- ✔ Coloring agents
- ✔ Curing agents
- ✔ Drying agents
- ✔ Emulsifiers

- ✔ Firming agents
- ✔ Flavor enhancers
- ✔ Flavoring agents
- ✔ Flour treating agents
- ✔ Formulation aids

133

- Humectants (promotes retention of water)
- Leavening agents
- Lubricants
- Nonnutritive sweeteners
- Nutritive Sweeteners
- Oxidizing and reducing agents
- pH control agents
- Processing aids
- Sequestrants
- Solvents, vehicles
- Stabilizers, thickeners
- Surface active agents
- Surface finishing agents
- Synergists
- Texturizers

44 SUBSTANCES TOXIC TO CATS

Any of these substances can harm or even kill your cat. Keep these away from your cat and demand a zero-tolerance policy for allowing your cat access to any of these toxins.

See the "Poisoning" section of the chapter "20 Common Cat Ailments and Their 14 Symptoms" for what symptoms to look for if you suspect your cat has been poisoned by one of the toxic substances listed below.

- Acetaminophen (Tylenol, etc.)
- Antifreeze
- Aspirin
- Azalea
- Bean plants
- Bleach
- Cactus
- Chocolate
- Crocus flowers
- Daffodil
- Drain cleaner
- Easter lilies
- Fertilizer of any kind
- Garlic
- Gasoline
- Hemlock
- Household cleaners (all!)
- Human medications and drugs
- Hydrangea
- Ibuprofen (Motrin, etc.)
- Insecticides and pesticides
- Ivy
- Kerosene
- Lead
- Marijuana
- Mistletoe
- Motor oil
- Mushrooms
- Nightshade
- Onions
- Over-the-counter vitamins for humans
- Paint of any kind
- Parsnip
- Phosphorous
- Poinsettia

- ✓ Poison Ivy
- ✓ Poison Oak
- ✓ Poison Sumac
- ✓ Poppies
- ✓ Rodenticide

- ✓ Tobacco products
- ✓ Tomato leaves
- ✓ Turpentine
- ✓ Walnuts

TREATMENT

If you suspect your cat has eaten something toxic, call your vet immediately or take your cat to the veterinary emergency room if you can get there quickly.

The Animal Poison Information Center is available 24 hours a day at 888-4ANI-HELP. There is a $45 charge per case.

Forced vomiting is not a good idea if your cat has ingested something like drain cleaner or acid or some other similarly corrosive substances. Vomiting this stuff back up will harm the cat's digestive tract and throat.

If your vet does ask you to induce vomiting, give your cat one or two teaspoons of ipecac syrup (which you should have in the house at all times). After your cat vomits, offer milk or water and watch your cat to see if he is drinking. If not, you may have to feed him fluids through a medicine syringe. Watch him carefully and get him to the vet if symptoms of poisoning persist.

"CAT CHAT" BY SARAH HARTWELL

Sarah Hartwell knows cats. She writes extensively and knowledgeably about felines and her work is published widely in magazines and on cat Web sites.

In this fascinating essay, Ms. Hartwell discusses "cat linguistics" and comes to the conclusion that even though our kitties may not actually be using "words" as we know the term; they do, indeed, make sounds to communicate a message—hunger, pain, affection, anger, and so on—to both their adopted humans and to other cats.

My cat Carter makes one specific sound—a kind of low-pitched rolling meow—what Sarah Hartwell would likely describe as an idiosyncratic sound, only when I am home, but somewhere away from him in an area of the house where he is not allowed to wander. My wife and I are convinced that this sound is my name in "Felinese." And I defy anyone to tell me otherwise. Ladies and Gentlemen: Sarah Hartwell.

🐾 🐾 🐾

CAT CHAT

Can cats talk? Many cat owners would like to think so and some even claim that their cats speak a number of recognisable words. A Brazilian cat takes claims one step further by apparently being able to sing a number of well known songs while the *Fortean Times* carried a report of a cat which speaks several words in Turkish and suggested, with tongue firmly in cheek, that the reason many owners cannot understand their cats is because the cats are speaking Turkish. But before cat-owners rush out for phrase books, are these cats really speaking or are their owners just talking turkey?

137

The cat's vocal apparatus differs from our own and is not designed with speech in mind. However, cats need to communicate, both with other cats and with owners. They "speak" to each other through body language, communicating feelings and intentions through posture and facial expression. In addition, they have a vocabulary of sounds ranging from caterwauls to mewing sounds, from hisses to the "silent meow" which is probably a sound pitched too high for human ears to hear. The familiar "miaow" is used mainly for communicating with humans as we are evidently too thick to understand anything other than kitten-talk.

DO CATS HAVE LANGUAGE?

In "Alice Through the Looking Glass," Lewis Carroll wrote "It is a very inconvenient habit of kittens that whatever you say to them, they always purr. If they would only purr for 'yes' and mew for 'no', or any rule of that sort, so that one could keep up a conversation! But how can one deal with a person if they always say the same thing?"

Lewis Carroll, it seems, was not a keen observer of cats, otherwise he would have noticed that cats do not always say the same thing! They make a variety of different sounds which, among humans would be called "words", but in our belief that we are naturally superior to "dumb" animals, we don't call cat-sounds "words". Since the sounds don't conform to our notion of grammatical structure, it simply appears that cats lack language.

To the uninitiated, and probably to Lewis Carroll, the simple "miaow" is an all-purpose word. Most cat-owners, however, are aware that there are a whole variety of miaows that differ in pitch, rhythm, volume, tone, and pronunciation. Jean Craighead George attempted to categorise these according to the cat's age, gender and situation:

KITTENS:

- Mew (high pitched and thin)—a polite plea for help.
- MEW! (loud and frantic)—an urgent plea for help.

ADULT CATS:

- Mew—plea for attention.
- Mew (soundless)—a very polite plea for attention (this is Paul Gallico's "Silent Miaow" which is probably a sound pitched too high for human ears).

- Meow—emphatic plea for attention.
- MEOW!—a command!
- Mee-o-ow (with falling cadence)—protest or whine.
- MEE-o-ow (shrill whine)—stronger protest.
- MYUP! (short, sharp, single note)—righteous indignation.
- MEOW! Meow! (repeated)—panicky call for help.
- Mier-r-r-ow (chirrup with lilting cadence)—friendly greeting.

TOMCATS:

- RR-YOWWW-EEOW-RR-YOW-OR—caterwaul.
- Merrow—challenge to another male.
- Meriow—courting call to female.

MOTHER CATS:

- MEE-OW—come and get it!.
- MeOW—follow me!.
- ME R-R-R-ROW—take cover!
- Mer ROW!—No! or Stop It!
- Mreeeep (burbled)—hello greeting to kittens and disarming greeting to adult cats (also used between adult cats and humans).

There is more to felinese that the simple miaow though. In 1944, Mildred Moelk made a detailed study of cat vocabulary and found 16 meaningful sounds, which included consonants and vowels. She divided cat-sounds into three groups:

- Murmurs made with the mouth closed.
- Vowel sounds made with the mouth closing as in "iao."
- Sounds made with the mouth held open.

Although these may not be used in grammatical sentences, one definition of language is "any means, vocal or other, of expressing or communicating feeling or thought" (Webster's Dictionary). Observant owners will notice the following sounds which cats make to communicate their state of mind (this list is not exhaustive, since cats will improvise):

- Caterwaul—cat wants sex!
- Chatter—excitement, frustration e.g. when prey is out of reach or escapes.
- Chirrup—friendly greeting sound, a cross between a meow and a purr!
- Cough-bark—alarm signal (rare in pet cats).

- ✔ Growl—threat, challenge, warns others to go away.
- ✔ Hiss (with or without spit)—threat, fear, warns others to back off.
- ✔ Meow—general-purpose attention seeking sound used by adult cats to communicate with owners or with kittens.
- ✔ Mew (of kittens)—distress, hunger, cold (to attract mother's attention).
- ✔ Purr—contentment, relaxation, also to comfort itself if in pain (cats in extremis may purr); a loud purr invites close contact or attention.
- ✔ Scream—fear, pain, anger, distress.
- ✔ Squawk—surprise, shock.
- ✔ Yowl—a threat, offensive or defensive, but also used in a modified form by some cats seeking attention when owner is out of sight
- ✔ Idiosyncratic sounds—a sound which a particular cat uses in a particular context.

The exact meanings of all of these sounds may be modified or emphasised by facial expression, tone/volume, body language, and context (paralanguage). In his dealings with Scottish Wildcats, Mike Tomkies noted that the wildcats would greet him with a loud spitting "PAAAH" accompanied by a foot-stamp. I have received the same greeting from feral cats. The meaning (" off!") is unmistakable and only a fool (or a cat-worker intent on packing pussy off for neutering) ignores it. Some cats may use some of these cat-sounds in different ways when communicating with humans and only our familiarity with our own pets tells us that a certain type of growl is a play noise and not warning of imminent attack.

Cat-owners will recognise many of the cat-sounds listed, although we may refer to them in more anthropomorphic terms: greet, grumble, nag, whimper, swear, sing, and so on. Some cats add their own idiosyncratic words to this general vocabulary such as the sudden exhalation of air used by my own cat, Aphrodite. This word, which we call "foof" or "frooff" can be anything from an exclamation ("Oh!" and "Well"), a comment ("So?" and "Huh?"), a non-committal response when we speak to her ("Hmmm"), or a noise to be used when she feels she needs to say something, but can't think of anything meaningful to say (small-talk and self-satisfied murmuring). It all depends on HOW it is said. For Aphrodite, "froof" is the all-purpose "supercalifragilistic..." of cat vocabulary. Scrapper used "mrrrp" in the same way.

LEARNING THE LINGO

Kittens learn a great deal from imitating their mother, and cats retain the ability to learn and adapt into their adult life. They soon discover that humans use sounds

Baker and Taylor prove that cats *do* understand English.

in order to communicate and most cats react to this by developing different sounds for certain circumstances. A plaintive miaow is best suited to achieving a goal such as extra grub or an open door while a friendly chirrup elicits a favourable response when the cat greets its owner. Many of these noises are accompanied by exaggerated actions as the cat "acts out" its communication—by running back and forth between owner and closed door or by licking invisible crumbs from an obviously empty food dish.

Humans have an innate language instinct and a need to communicate vocally (or through sign language etc.) with everyone about them. Adults with small children use a simplified version of language known as baby-talk (called "motherese" by some linguists) where certain words and syllables are greatly stressed and frequently repeated. These efforts are rewarded when baby makes noises back and parents readily identify meaningful noises ("mum-mum") in their babies when the rest of us hear only random babble. In response, parents talk even more to their offspring.

Whether or not we consider our cats to be surrogate children, we tend to relate to them in a similar way, using motherese to communicate with them. Cats may respond to this verbal barrage by making noises of their own. After all, if their humans need to communicate through all this audible chit-chat, any self-respecting cat is going to have to make noises if it is to stand any chance of getting attention!

And since the owner lacks much of the necessary apparatus needed for speaking felinese (tail, mobile ears, whiskers, erectile fur) it is up to the cat to learn humanese.

One feature common to both cats and people is the use of a slightly raised tone of voice to indicate friendliness and a lowered tone of voice to indicate displeasure, aggression etc. Friendly chirrup and food-seeking miaow are usually uttered in a raised tone of voice while the low-pitched growl of a cross cat is undeniably unfriendly. Volume is sometimes used for added emphasis e.g. a strident miaow for urgency, a gentle "brrp" for contentment. Cats which simply feel compelled to add their two penn'orth to a conversation often do so in a neutral tone of voice to indicate that they are not being particularly hostile, nor unduly friendly, nor is there any great urgency about the subject matter.

CAN CATS TALK PEOPLE-TALK?

Humans have an instinctive need to communicate with fellow humans and to receive communication in return. This drive is often extended to our interaction with non-humans. Just as we look for recognisable sounds when babies learn to talk, we look for recognisable sounds in our cats' "vocabulary." Rather than simply distinguishing a "feed me" miaow from a "let me out please" miaow, we try to interpret some of these sounds as words and are remarkably good at self-deception. So if the "I want more grub" noise sounds a bit like "keow" we think our cat is calling us a cow for not giving it a big enough helping in the first place. Cats which "talk" are probably making native feline sounds that sound a little like human words and which, if delivered under the right circumstances, are interpreted as words by beings geared to verbal communication.

I say probably, because here there is a slightly grey area. According to American vet Dr Michael W. Fox cats can learn behaviours through observation. My own observations suggest that some cats learn to imitate certain sounds as well. Cats can make sounds and work out which sounds elicit suitable responses from humans (positive feedback). Can cats therefore learn to make certain sounds i.e. imitate certain human sounds if they know it will get a favourable response? Here I will have to give cats the benefit of the doubt. It may be that, in spite of lacking the apparatus for speech, some cats do indeed make the effort. Equally, it may be that owners are over-compensating for the cat's inability to talk and are hearing what they want to hear, regardless of what the cat has really said!

Another feature of human speech is that it comes in bursts; a mix of different sounds and pauses between sounds, plus inflection and intonation. Tone of voice probably means as much to a cat than the actual words used, although many owners maintain that their cat understands every word they say. Cats certainly manage intonation and can miaow in a questioning manner, a demanding manner, a forlorn manner, or simply as a statement. By observing our response, they adopt the various tones of miaow for appropriate circumstances. Puss probably isn't thinking, "I want to go out so I shall ask nicely," he is more likely to be thinking "I want to go and I know that this type of noise usually does the trick."

In their attempts to communicate with us on our own level, some cats put together full "sentences" of noises and pauses. They might simply be inviting us to talk back to them (most cats like this sort of attention from their owners). It is interesting that such cats string together a series of different sounds into a single burst of communication, with pauses between "words", which an owner likens to a sentence. Scrapper (one of felinity's brighter sparks) could hold his own in a conversation with me although I haven't a clue what he was saying, he just liked to talk and liked me to talk back. If he did understand what I was saying to him he could have taken the Business Studies exam with me (if he was trying to enlighten me on a particular aspect of management structure, then I'm afraid it went right over my head). Some owners say that their cats do much the same and are right chatterboxes, with Siamese and Oriental cats being particularly vocal.

I doubt very much that cats, those from C.S. Lewis's *Narnia* excepted, can truly speak, although cat-sounds are more diverse and more meaningful than Lewis Caroll suggests. What I don't doubt is that there are a number of cats having a jolly good attempt—whether in Turkish or any other tongue. What is worrying though, is when I am doing the evening shift at a cat shelter and I am convinced that I can hear someone talking, even though there are no other humans, only cats, in the vicinity. So far none of the cats have owned up!

(My thanks go to Prof Mark Woodroffe, lecturer at Anglia Polytechnic University, Essex, for stimulating my interest in linguistics. I don't think he believed me when I told him that cats could talk!)

21 FACTS ABOUT YOUR CAT'S SENSES

SIGHT, SMELL, HEARING, TASTE, AND TOUCH

🐾 A cat can see colors but they do not see them as vivid as humans do. Scientific experiments have confirmed that cats can differentiate between the following pairs of colors:
- Blue and gray.
- Green and blue.
- Green and gray.
- Red and blue.
- Red and gray.
- Red and green.
- Yellow and blue.
- Yellow and gray.

🐾 A cat sees the world the way a human with a cataract does—a little blurry and soft around the edges.

🐾 Cats need one-sixth of the light humans do to see movement.

🐾 Cats do not like high-pitched, vibrating noises, like the whine of a garbage disposal or a vacuum cleaner, or some of the most annoying alarm clock sounds. (But then again, who does?)

🐾 A cat's taste buds are on the tip, sides, and base of their tongue.

🐾 A cat's tongue is as sensitive as the skin on its nose and pads of its paws.

🐾 If a cat sneers, it is probably bringing more air to its Jacobcon's organ, which is found on the roof of its

145

Missy demonstrates every cat's sixth sense: sleep.

mouth. This organ allows the cat to differentiate between odors and enhance its smelling abilities. (The term for this expression is flehming.)

- A cat's whiskers are tremendously sensitive and can register even the slightest touch. Cats often use their whiskers for navigation in the dark.

- A cat's ears can rotate and move in a wide range of directions and each ear has 30 muscles that a cat uses to move its ears to pick up even the slightest of sounds.

- Cats can hear exceptionally high frequency sounds, up to 65 kilohertz. The maximum a human can hear is 20 kilohertz.

- Kittens are born blind and do not open their eyes until they are between 8 and 20 days old.

- In dim light, a cat's pupil can dilate enormously and almost completely fill the cat's iris. In bright light, the pupil can contract to a thin line to protect the cat's eye.

- A cat has 30 teeth (and they're sharp, as any cat owner who has been on the receiving end of a cat bite can attest to). However, cats cannot chew.

- A cat possesses an extraordinary sense of balance, which is controlled by the semicircular canals in its inner ears.

- A cat has three eyelids.

- Cats spend 30 percent of their waking hours grooming themselves.

- Light makes cats shed. Cats shed most in the summer and even electric lights and the light from a TV can make a cat shed.

- Cats sleep 16 hours a day.

- Cats do not walk on their paws—they walk on their claws, and they are the only clawed animal on earth to do so.

- Cats can predict earthquakes.

- It is almost impossible for a human being to retrieve a cat from under a bed if a cat does not choose to be retrieved.

9 MYTHS AND FACTS ABOUT CATS

Are these statements true or false?

- ✔ Cats always land on their feet.
- ✔ Cats should drink milk every day.

The correct answer to both is **false**.

These are common misunderstandings that veterinarians frequently hear from pet owners, according to the American Animal Hospital Association (AAHA).

Following is a list of popular myths that AAHA veterinarians and The Cat Fanciers' Association (CFA) would like to dispel:

Myth: Cats always land on their feet.

Fact: While cats instinctively fall feet first and may survive falls from high places, they also may receive broken bones in the process. Some kind of screening on balconies and windows can help protect pets from disastrous falls.

Myth: Cats should drink milk every day.

Fact: Most cats like milk, but do not need it if properly nourished. Also, many will get diarrhea if they drink too much milk. If it is given at all, the amount should be small and infrequent.

Myth: Cats that are spayed or neutered automatically gain weight.

Fact: Like people, cats gain weight from eating too much, not exercising enough, or both. In many cases, spaying or neutering is done at an age when the animal's metabolism already has slowed, and its need for food has decreased. If the cat continues to eat the same amount, it may gain weight. Cat owners can help their cats stay fit by providing exercise and not over-feeding.

Myth: Cats cannot get rabies.

Fact: Actually, most warm-blooded mammals, including cats, bats, skunks, and ferrets, can carry rabies. Like dogs, cats should be vaccinated regularly according to local laws.

Myth: Indoor cats cannot get diseases.

Fact: Cats still are exposed to organisms that are carried through the air or brought in on a cat owner's shoes or clothing. Even the most housebound cat ventures outdoors at some time, and can be exposed to diseases and worms through contact with other animals' feces.

Myth: Tapeworms come from bad food.

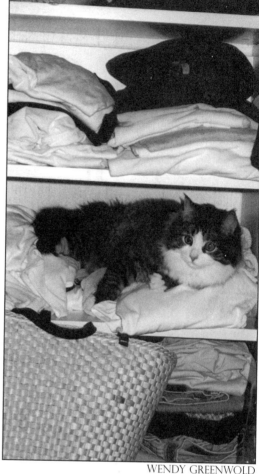
WENDY GREENWOLD
Myth: Cats are very comfortable undergarments.

Fact: Pets become infected with tapeworms from swallowing fleas, which carry the parasite. Also, cats can get tapeworms from eating infected mice or other exposed animals.

Myth: Putting garlic on a pet's food will get rid of worms.

Fact: Garlic may make the animal's food taste better but has no effect on worms. The most effective way to treat worms is by medication prescribed by a veterinarian.

Myth: Pregnant women should not own cats.

Fact: Some cats can be infected with a disease called toxoplasmosis, which occasionally can be spread to humans through cat litter boxes and cause serious problems in unborn babies. However, these problems can be controlled, if the expectant mother avoids contact with the litter box and assigns daily cleaning to a friend or other family member.

Myth: A cat's sense of balance is in its whiskers.

Fact: Cats use their whiskers as "feelers" to determine widths, but not to maintain their balance.

Myth: Animals heal themselves by licking their wounds.

Fact: Such licking actually can slow the healing process and further damage the wound.

🐾 🐾 🐾

For the most accurate information on these and other concerns about pet health care, the American Animal Hospital Association and The Cat Fanciers' Association advise cat owners to contact a veterinarian.

The AAHA is an international association of more than 12,000 veterinarians who treat companion animals, such as cats and dogs. The association is well-known among veterinarians for its high standards for hospitals and pet health care.

The CFA is the world's largest registry of pedigreed cats and has reaffirmed its commitment to the promotion of the welfare of ALL cats, pedigreed or random bred.

The Winn Feline Foundation was founded in 1968 by CFA as a source of funding for medical studies benefiting cats. The Winn Foundation has provided funds over the years for a wide variety of studies and has helped to advance veterinary knowledge in all areas of feline health. Grants totaling more than $1.2 million have been awarded by the Winn Foundation since its inception. For additional information on CFA, AAHA or the Winn Foundation, please contact:

The Cat Fanciers' Association, Inc.

1805 Atlantic Avenue

PO Box 1005

Manasquan NJ 08736-0805

Phone: 732-528-9797

Fax: 732-528-7391

American Animal Hospital Association

12575 W. Bayaud Avenue

Lakewood, CO 80228

303-986-2800

www.healthypet.com

American Animal Hospital Association
Derek Woodbury
Public Relations Manager
800-252-2242
www.aahanet.org

The Winn Feline Foundation
1805 Atlantic Avenue
PO Box 1005
Manasquan NJ 08736-0805
Phone: 732-528-9797

10 CAT QUESTIONS WITH "SURVIVOR'S" KIMMI KAPPENBERG

*"I have no regrets, whatsoever.
I would never eat a cow brain.
I wouldn't change anything,
and I had to be true to myself."*

—from Kimmi's Final chat (complete transcript available at:
survivor.cbs.com/primetime/survivor2/survivors/kimmi_c1.html.)

O f all the myriad, motley, mesmerizing, and maddening castaways on *Survivor II*, there was really only one whom I wanted to talk to for this book: Kimmi the vegetarian—the Long Island bartender, writer, and production assistant who befriended a chicken and was willing to risk her tribe losing a reward challenge rather than eat a serving of yummy cow brains.

Kimmi ultimately did eat a worm (yuck) and win the challenge for her tribe, but she made it very clear throughout her three or so weeks on the show that she was a passionate vegetarian and animal lover (and that she

CBS WORLDWIDE INC.

Kimmi Kappenberg.

wasn't too crazy about Alicia, either). When her tribe won two chickens and a rooster, Kimmi could be heard warning Roger to be careful that he did not break her wings as he put the chicken in a box.

Here is Kimmi's official CBS biography, followed by our interview. At the conclusion of our "10 Questions" are Kimmi's final words after being voted off the island (which, in season 2, was the "island" of Australia!) in Episode 5.

Kimmi Kappenberg currently works as a bartender in Long Island, New York, while also freelancing as a production assistant for television commercials. Having taken courses at Suffolk Community

153

College, University of Houston, and Stephen F. Austin State University, she ultimately received a Bachelor of Arts degree from the New York Institute of Technology. She is most proud of the fact that she graduated at the top of her class after having taken a few years off from school.

Kappenberg describes herself as spontaneous, outgoing, and creative. Her favorite hobbies are photography, gardening, and reading. Her perfect day would include a trip to the beach, horseback riding, eating many times (a vegetarian, she will not eat land-dwelling animals, only seafood), having sex, and watching the sunset. Her favorite television shows are *Win Ben Stein's Money* and *The Simpsons*, while her favorite motion pictures are *Cruel Intentions* and *Beauty and the Beast*. She prefers country, 80s, and club music. Her favorite sports team is the New York Yankees and she prefers a good game of Trivial Pursuit or Scrabble when she has time.

Born and raised in East Setauket, Long Island, Kappenberg currently resides in Ronkonkoma, Long Island. Currently single, she lives with her cat, Abbi, while her other three cats, Bart, Sasha, and Meow, and her twin Shih Tzu dogs, Till and Fievel, live with her parents. Her birth date is November 11.

Author's note: Kimmi was on the road doing a slew of PR media interviews when I asked her for an interview for this book, and she very kindly managed to squeeze in "talking" to me (via e-mail, of course!) while in hotels and in the midst of traveling all over the place for *Survivor* appearances. I greatly appreciate her generosity with her time and for allowing me to complete the interview so quickly. Thanks, Kimmi. You rock!

🐾 🐾 🐾

Stephen Spignesi: How many cats do you have and what are their names? Do you have a favorite?

Kimmi Kappenberg: I have four. One lives with me, Abbi. She adopted me last May when she was about three weeks old. My 18-year-old cat Meow, 10-year-old Bart, and 8-year-old Sasha moved to upstate New York when my parents retired because finding an apartment in New York that would allow them was rough.

SS: Are they indoor or outdoor cats?

KK: Abbi stays indoors, claws and all. Bart and Sasha come in and out whenever they want. They are declawed, which was not my doing. Meow was an indoor cat when I rescued her 12 years ago. She was always allowed to venture outside but now just usually hangs around on window sills or on a deck sunning herself by a garden.

SS: Who cared for your cats when you were on *Survivor?*

KK: My parents had the usual three and my brother let Abbi move in.

SS: Where do you stand on the declawing issue?

KK: I'm not for declawing. Two of mine are declawed and go outside and still get in fights with other cats. Bart is famous for killing mice, moles, bunnies, and snakes and he climbs trees, all without claws so the whole "they can't defend themselves outside when they are declawed" is a farce. My cats will not be deprived of the outside even if they are declawed. As I said, declawing them wasn't my doing.

SS: Personally, I believe cats are psychic. Can your cats read your thoughts? How do they communicate with you so you know what they want?

KK: Cats are very sensitive and always have a way of knowing when times are bad for me. I had a cat Ashley who I hate to admit was my favorite. She was with me from when I was about six years old to about 24. This cat was the most sensitive and loving creature. Abbi and I are very close. I guess because she found me when she was only a couple of weeks old and I am the person she has the most contact with. She is very sensitive to my feelings. She knows when it's play time and she knows when it's just time to cuddle. She just walked over to me typing this, she must know I'm talking about her!

SS: I've been a vegetarian for almost 20 years and remember the day I made the decision to stop eating meat completely, as well as the incident that precipitated the decision. How long have you been a vegetarian and what made you decide to stop eating meat?

KK: I never really had a fondness for meat. When I did eat it, it had to have zero trace of blood, like shoe leather. When I was in the 2nd or 3rd grade, my class went to a farm to see the animals. I played with some pigs, and then my mother made pork chops that night, which, to me, was just plain wrong! As I got older, it continued to bother me, and when I was around 12, I pretty much stopped eating pork, lamb, and beef. Then at 17 I gave up poultry. I just couldn't look at a cow and then be at peace with eating it. It is a nurturing mammal that nurses its young, the same as people. It has a familial bond, and I'm not going to be responsible for breaking that. I'm a fake veggie, though, because I do occasionally have fish. At least fish are not factory farmed and most of them can be eaten raw. I strongly believe that if humans were meant to eat meat, then we wouldn't have to cook it for fear of contracting a disease.

SS: There's an old saying about the personalities of pets that states that dogs are like children and cats are like adults. Do you agree with this? Why or why not?

KK: I've never heard this, but I guess it could be true. Dogs are always sticking their noses in things and wanting to know about everything that is new, whereas cats like simplicity more. My cats always just love sitting in a garden or in the window feeling the sun, the way an older person would enjoy a lemonade on a porch swing. Dogs and children are always running around while cats and elders are usually mellow—but watch out for them when they find something they like, like a leaf, and Bingo! they'll get feisty really quick.

CBS WORLDWIDE INC.
Kimmi the mermaid.

SS: You obviously are one of those people who are able to bond with animals. This was obvious from the chicken and pig incidents on the show. One of the most painful ordeals I have ever had to go through was having to put to sleep a beloved cat that I had had for 16 years. Have you ever had to go through this, and, if so, could you talk about your feelings and how you dealt with it?

KK: When Ashley died a few years ago, I took it really hard. Her birthday was April 1st, and I always gave her a can of good tuna or something special, sang happy birthday to her...all the happy sappy stuff. She had always been this all-white frisky furball. Her last few weeks were horrible. Every day I'd come home and ask, "Where's Ashley?" and Mom would say, here, or there, or wherever. Well, one day I came home and Ashley meowed at me, and she just looked so thin. I laid on the floor with her and she just purred at me and let me hold her. I got her a can of tuna and drained the juice for her to lap, but she didn't even want that. I knew she was getting ready to leave. The next day I came home, walked around and said, "Where's Ashley?" My parents looked at me with their faces all swollen from crying and told me she never came back inside after they let her out that morning. I cried for a week; I was sick to my stomach. I looked for her body all over but never found it. That first day I was so mad at my mother for letting her out, knowing that she was going to die, but Ashley needed to do what was best for her.

SS: Could you describe how being on *Survivor* has changed your life?

KK: Survivor gave me more self confidence, and it reaffirmed that it's okay to go against the group. I can rely on myself more than I thought. *Survivor* also showed the world only some of my personality, not everything about me. It is a bit of an adjustment walking around and having strangers think that they know me. It is different than being an actor. I wasn't playing a role. I was myself, so people really think they know everything about who I am.

SS: One last *Survivor* question: When this book comes out, everyone will know who won *Survivor II*. Are you pleased or displeased with who won?

KK: Right this moment (mid-April 2001) all of us only know the last two people. We all find out together who wins at the final episode, so I can't answer that now! (Note: It was Tina.)

SS: Fair enough! Thanks for taking the time to talk to us, Kimmi.

KK: You're welcome, Steve, and good luck with the book!

KIMMI'S FINAL WORDS ON "SURVIVOR II"

Well, it was a game, and twelve out of 50,000 is not a bad thing. Little sad, but glad that I stayed true to myself and my morals. Hope I didn't let my family down too much by getting booted off so soon, but I definitely had a great, great time, and it's okay! It's okay 'cause I got lots waiting for me on the other side.

I knew for a long time that my head was on the chopping block, so it doesn't surprise me at all. But, you get a little disappointed; you would have liked to have been here longer. But I definitely, definitely knew. I know that Alicia and I have not gotten along since day one. I know she's made friendships with a lot of other people, whereas I've spent more time with myself. But I need that for me—to be with myself. And I expected it. But you know, if that's what they felt that they had to do, then—you know—power to the team!

I think that…I guess there was a lot of persuasion. I mean, just because I do spend a lot of time on my own. Maybe the team feels isolated. Like, I didn't partake in the pig hunt. I don't have chicken. You know what I mean? So there's a lot of things where I'm separate just because of food or whatever, but…I'm just a little bit separate.

48 LEGENDS AND SUPERSTITIONS ABOUT CATS

*"Can you look out the window
Without your shadow getting in the way?
Oh, you're so beautiful
With an edge and a charm..."*

—Sarah McLachlan

There are nowhere near as many superstitions and legends about dogs as there are about cats. The aura of mystery and uncompromising inscrutability of the cat has resulted in a fascinating litter of myths about these amazing animals. (The theater may be one of the only categories that rival cats as a source for superstitions, myths, and legends.)

This list of 48 cat legends and superstitions range from the mundane—No. 17: "A sneezing cat brings good luck"; to the unspeakably bizarre—No. 37: "Serious wounds and injuries can be treated by applying a poultice made from a whole cat boiled in olive oil."

This collection spans the globe, from Europe and the Middle East to the American South and elsewhere. (This list complements quite nicely the informative essay that follows: "Cat Omens and Oracles" by High Priestess of the Old Religion Gerina Dunwich.)

Disclaimer: The author and publishers of The Cat Book of Lists *do not endorse any of these beliefs, and hope that it does not need to be actually stated (although we'll state it anyway) that no one should actually attempt or carry out any of the acts detailed in this collection of often ridiculous superstitions (especially the ones involving bodily harm to a feline), all of which are presented here purely for entertainment and scholarly purposes.*

1. Sorcerers are believed to be able to turn themselves into black cats.

2. Black cats feed on the blood of their witch mistresses.

3. A kitten born in May should be immediately drowned. (Because, of course, May is the month most associated with death.)

4. It is dangerous to discuss personal family matters in front of a cat, because the cat may be a witch's familiar (attendant spirit) who may take the information back to her mistress who will then use it against you.

159

5. If you mark a cat with a cross, it will prevent it from turning into a witch.

6. A cat suspected of being a witch should be caged and burned alive as soon as possible.

7. In Europe, a black cat that crosses a person's path miraculously bestows upon that person one wish, which most likely will be granted.

8. To get rid of all your warts, kill a cat and bury it in a black stocking.

9. In the United States, Spain, and Belgium, a black cat that crosses a person's path will bring terrible bad luck.

10. A black cat that turns to look back at you is an omen of dire things to come.

11. A black cat seen from behind will bring bad luck.

12. Touching a black cat will bring good luck.

13. White cats are feared and distrusted in Europe.

14. Stray tortoiseshell cats will bring bad luck into the home that welcomes them.

15. If you use money to pay for a cat, the cat will never be a good mousecatcher.

16. If a cat sneezes, it is going to rain.

17. A sneezing cat brings good luck.

18. If a cat sneezes three times everyone in the house will get a cold.

19. A cat that sits with its back to a fire is a prediction of cold weather.

20. A cat that sits with its back to a fire is a prediction of a storm.

21. If a cat scratches the leg of a table, the weather is going to change.

22. If a cat cavorts and carouses, wet weather is on its way.

23. If a cat washes himself while sitting in a doorway, a member of the clergy will soon visit.

24. If a cat washes its face by rubbing its paw over its left ear, a women or a girl will arrive soon for a visit.

25. If a cat washes its face by rubbing its paw over its left ear, a man will soon arrive.

26. If a cat stands next to a bride, good luck will come to the newlyweds.

27. If a cat jumps over a coffin, it must be captured and killed, since it may have stolen the soul of the deceased, thereby preventing a smooth passage to the next world.

28. If you kill a cat, you will be sacrificing your soul to the Devil.

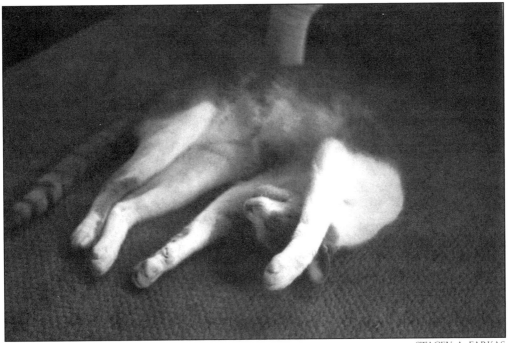

Cat superstition #523.7: Putting your paw over your head makes you invisible.

29. If you kick a cat, you will develop rheumatism.

30. Cats can suck the breath out of an infant while it's sleeping and kill him.

31. If you draw a cat's tail across your eye, it will cure a sty.

32. If you drag a cat's tail across a wart in the month of May, the wart will disappear.

33. You can relieve a toothache by pressing a dried catskin on your face over the afflicted tooth.

34. Serious wounds and injuries can be treated by applying a poultice made from a whole cat boiled in olive oil.

35. You can cure tuberculosis by eating a gravy made from a stewed black cat.

36. Many illnesses can be cured by washing the patient and then throwing the dirty water on top of a cat. The belief is that the water contains the illness and that the cat will take the sickness with him when it runs out of the house (which it most certainly will) after getting doused.

37. A cat that jumps up onto the lap of a pregnant woman might kill her unborn child.

38. It is bad luck to say "cat" when working in a mine, and even worse luck to allow a cat down into a mine.

39. Black cats are good luck on sea voyages.

40. A crying cat onboard a ship is a portent of bad times on their way.

41. If a cat plays excitedly onboard a ship, a big wind is coming.

42. If a cat is mistreated onboard a ship or, heaven forfend, thrown overboard, everyone on board will be immediately punished by a catastrophic storm.

43. If you lock a cat in a cupboard, you will summon a dangerous wind.

44. If you trap a cat under a pot, you will summon a dangerous wind.

45. If the wife of a sailor keeps a black cat at home while her husband is out at sea, he will have good luck on his voyage.

46. If your pet canary is killed by a cat you do not know, you will suffer two years of bad luck.

47. If a black cat you do not know "adopts" you and chooses to make its home with you, you will have only good luck for as long as the cat lives with you.

48. A grease made from a wild cat will cure back and leg disabilities.

"CAT OMENS AND ORACLES" BY GERINA DUNWICH

Cats have long been looked to as harbingers of the future, and High Priestess of the Old Religion, Gerina Dunwich, is a world-renowned authority on felidomancy (she'll tell you what that is in a moment) as well as many other occult and Wicca traditions and practices. Here, in an essay written exclusively for *The Cat Book of Lists*, Dunwich discusses the progonosticatory abilities of one of mankind's favorite companion animals. Special thanks to Gerina Dunwich for providing her insight and wisdom to my readers.—SJS

Gerina Dunwich.

🐈 🐈 🐈

The formal name for the art and practice of divination by the behavior and actions of both domestic and wild cats is felidomancy (which is Latin for "divination by felines"). It is related to zoomancy (divination by the observation of animal behavior); however, it should not be confused with the divinatory method known as apantomancy, which draws omens from chance meetings with animals or birds (such as the popular foretelling of bad luck by a black cat crossing one's path).

Diviners throughout the world have used cats to predict the future since antiquity. Felidomancy was known to have been practiced in ancient Egypt, where the feline was deified and worshipped for many centuries. Temple priests and diviners used special cats, adorned with precious jewels and magickal symbols, in a variety of ways to unlock the mysteries of the future. Cat divination was especially significant when it concerned the fates of the pharaohs and even Egypt herself.

Felidomancy was also a popular practice in ancient Greece, Rome, Persia (now called Iran), Northern Europe, India, Phoenicia (now Syria and Lebanon), China, and Japan. Cat divination became widespread throughout Europe and the British Isles by the early part of the Middle Ages.

It was once a common practice for farmers in Europe to determine the success or failure of their future harvests by dropping a live cat from the top of the bell tower of a church. A good harvest was portended if the cat landed on its feet. If the cat landed on any other part of its body and survived, the farmers believed that this was a sign of a difficult year ahead. However, if the cat died as a result of the fall or of any bodily injuries sustained by it, this was taken as a warning of crop failure by drought, blight, or even sorcery.

Felidomancy has also been practiced in connection with affairs of the heart. In the Victorian era, women who were unsure whether or not they should accept a marriage proposal from a particular suitor utilized a popular method known as "leaving it to the cat". It called for three hairs to be plucked from the tail of a pure white cat and then placed within a folded piece of paper, which would be placed underneath the doorstep at the stroke of midnight. Come the next dawn, the paper would be carefully unfolded and the hairs examined. If they were found to cross each other, this was a sign that marriage proposal should be accepted. But if the hairs failed to cross, it was in the woman's best interest to turn it down and wait for the next one.

If a bride should see a sneezing cat on the day of her wedding, this is said to be a very good omen, portending a happy marriage blessed with love and fidelity. If a strange white cat should come to the house and sun itself on the doorstep, this is an omen that a member of the family will soon be getting married. However, a black cat that shows up on the doorstep of a woman or man on the morning of their wedding day is believed by some to be a very unlucky omen warning to postpone the wedding at once or call it off all together.

It was believed long ago in Germany that the cat was a harbinger of death. If a black cat jumped onto the bed of a sickly person, or if an elderly or gravely ill person witnessed two cats hissing and clawing at each other, this was said to be an omen of that individual's death.

If a cat is seen washing its face over its left ear, this is a sign that a woman will soon come to call. If a cat washes its face over its right ear, the caller will be a man. In some parts of the United States it is believed that when a cat washes itself in a doorway, this portends a visit from a man of the cloth.

One modern and simple method of cat divination is to concentrate upon a particular yes-or-no question, and then write it thrice upon a piece of parchment. Whisper the name of your cat nine times to yourself and then ask your question three times out loud. After doing so, call to your cat, which will act as an oracle. An affirmative answer is indicated if the cat enters the room by its right forepaw first. If it enters by its left forepaw first, the answer to your question is negative.

Black cats have long been regarded as omens of bad luck in the United States, Ireland, Spain, and Belgium. However, in the British Isles and many parts of Europe, they are regarded as omens of good luck, while white cats are looked upon as the harbingers of misfortune. Some people believe that calico cats (especially male ones, which are extremely rare) bring good fortune and even possess healing powers. But the luckiest of all cats are said to be those possessing a double set of claws.

Using the behavior of a cat to predict the weather is perhaps the oldest and most popular use of felidomancy. It continues to be practiced in modern times, especially in rural regions of Europe and Great Britain where many individuals continue to follow the old traditional ways and beliefs of the generations before them. In the United States, where cat divination is most popular in the southern regions and in the Ozarks, remnants of felidomancy in the form of common weather omens can be found alive and well in both rural areas and big cities alike.

If the tail of a sleeping calico cat is turned toward the north or east, this is said to be a sign of an approaching storm. But if it is turned toward a southern or western direction, fair weather is portended. Many country folks say that when a cat washes behind its ears with a wet paw, sits with its tail turned toward the fireplace, or lies curled up with its forehead touching the ground, the chances are good that a storm will soon be brewing. Some people also believe that a cat that sits with its back to the fireplace portends the coming of cold weather or a hard frost.

It is said that rainy weather is in the offing when a cat sneezes or licks its tail. A cat that scratches a table leg with its claws or washes vigorously behind its ears also indicates a change in the weather.

In China it was once believed that the winking of a cat's eye could predict rain. If a cat on board a ship acted unusually playful and frolicsome, Chinese seafarers were convinced that this was a sign of an impending gale. This old belief is reflected in a cat rhyme from the 18th century Poetical Description of Beasts, which goes: "Against the times of snow or hail, Or boist'rous windy storms; She frisks about and wags her tail, And many tricks performs."

An old weather superstition from the state of Maine holds that if a cat washes its face in the parlor or sharpens its claws upon a fence, expect a downpour. Some New England fishermen still believe that if a cat behaves in any sort of peculiar or nervous manner, this is a warning of an approaching tempest.

But if a cat should quietly contemplate the face of the moon, this is a sign that the next day shall see weather most fair.

🐈 🐈 🐈

Gerina Dunwich is a High Priestess of the Old Religion, a professional astrologer, a lifelong student of the occult, and a cat-lover. Ordained as a minister by the Universal Life Church, she is the founder of the Bast-Wicca tradition of the Craft, and the author of the following books:

- *Candlelight Spells*
- *The Cauldron of Dreams*
- *Circle of Shadows*
- *The Concise Lexicon of the Occult*
- *Everyday Wicca*
- *Exploring Spellcraft*
- *Herbal Magick* (forthcoming)
- *Magick Potions*
- *The Pagan Book of Halloween*
- *Priestess and Pentacle*
- *Wicca A to Z*
- *The Wicca Book of Days*
- *Wicca Candle Magick*
- *Wicca Craft*
- *A Wiccan's Dictionary of Prophecy and Omens*
- *The Wicca Garden*
- *Wicca Love Spells*
- *The Wicca Sourcebook*
- *The Wicca Spellbook*
- *Your Magickal Cat*

8 CHINESE "YEARS OF THE CAT"

Chinese astrology assigns a patron animal to each year and the cat is one of these mystical designees. There were eight "Years of the Cat" in the 20th Century in America and here is a look at those auspicious years and some of the events that occurred in each. We leave it to you to decide whether having a year christened a "cat year" portends good or bad fortune for those who lived through it.

YEAR OF THE CAT 1903

- The Wright Brothers make their first sustained manned flight.
- The Harley-Davidson motorcycle is introduced.
- "Typhoid Mary" infects New York with 1,300 cases of typhoid fever.
- Marconi sends a wireless message 3,000 miles.
- The first World Series is played (Boston beats Pittsburgh 5 games to 3).
- Sanka Coffee is introduced.
- The Pepsi-Cola name is trademarked.

167

- The New York Stock Exchange building is built.
- It is discovered that x-rays (radiation) can inhibit the growth of cancer cells.
- The Supreme Court upholds a clause in the Alabama Constitution denying blacks the right to vote.

YEAR OF THE CAT 1915

- World War I (known at this time as the Great War) intensifies dramatically.
- The Germans use chlorine gas at Ypres, marking the first time poison gas is used in warfare.
- German torpedoes sink the *Lusitania*.
- The Tommy Gun (the Thompson submachine gun) is introduced.
- The Ku Klux Klan is formed in Georgia.
- Long-distance telephone service from New York to San Francisco begins (a call takes 23 minutes to go through and costs $20.70).

- The mechanical pencil is invented.
- Processed cheese is invented by Kraft.
- Perhaps in response to the creation of processed cheese, Kellogg's introduces 40 percent Bran Flakes breakfast cereal.
- Pyrex glass is invented.

YEAR OF THE CAT 1927

- Italians Nicola Sacco and Bartolomeo Vanzetti are electrocuted for murder, even though they are innocent.
- Charles Lindbergh successfully completes the first solo transatlantic flight.
- The Iron Lung is invented.
- Transatlantic telephone service begins.
- Television is first demonstrated in New York at the Bell Laboratories.
- The Academy of Motion Picture Arts and Sciences is founded.
- The first all-electric jukeboxes are introduced.
- Babe Ruth hits his historic 60th home run.

- Crime lord Al Capone earns $105 million, the highest gross income of an American citizen to date.
- The Mississippi River floods in April, covering 4 million acres and cause $300 million in damages.
- Wonder Bread is introduced.

YEAR OF THE CAT 1939

- World War II begins.
- The U.S. unemployment rate is a staggering 17 percent.
- General Electric introduces fluorescent lighting.
- Nylon is invented.
- Howard Hughes buys TWA.
- FM radios go on sale for the first time.
- Batman is created by 18-year-old Bob Kane.
- James Joyce publishes *Finnegan's Wake*.
- The Baseball Hall of Fame is established at Cooperstown, New York.
- Cup-sizing for brassieres is introduced.
- Pall Mall introduces the first "king-size" cigarette.
- The U.S. Department of Agriculture launches the Food Stamp program.
- Birds Eye begins selling the first frozen foods—a chicken fricassee dinner and "criss-cross" Steak.

YEAR OF THE CAT 1951

- The Korean War rages.
- The world's first thermonuclear bomb is set off by the United States on the Pacific island of Eniwetok.
- Chrysler begins installing power steering in its Crown Imperial sedans.
- "Dennis the Menace" is launched in 16 newspapers.
- CBS Television begins broadcasting in color.

- J.D. Salinger publishes *The Catcher in the Rye*.
- Mickey Mantle joins the Yankees.
- The worst floods in U.S. history drown Kansas and Missouri; damages total $1 billion.
- The United States loans India $190 million to buy American grain.
- Gerber begins using MSG in baby food.

YEAR OF THE CAT 1963

- President John F. Kennedy is assassinated in Dallas, Texas.
- Martin Luther King Jr. delivers his "I have a dream" speech in Washington, D.C.
- The Supreme Court rules that "if you cannot afford an attorney, one will be provided for you at no cost."
- New Hampshire launches the first ever state lottery.
- Half of the United States' federal budget of $100 billion goes for military appropriations for our involvement in Southeast Asia.
- An artificial heart is used during heart surgery for the first time.
- Valium is introduced.
- Touch-Tone phones are introduced.
- Betty Friedan publishes *The Feminine Mystique*.
- The Beatles release "I Want To Hold Your Hand."
- Weight Watchers is founded.
- Tab is introduced.

YEAR OF THE CAT 1975

- The United States evacuates all forces from Vietnam.
- John Mitchell, H.R. Haldeman, and John Erlichman are sentenced to prison for their roles in the Watergate cover-up.
- The first U.S./Soviet space linkup takes place.
- President Ford signs the Metric Conversion Act; Americans ignore it.
- Microsoft is founded at Seattle by 19-year-old Bill Gates and his partner Paul Allen.
- Laboratory-created monoclonal antibodies are first used in the treatment of disease.

- Lyme Disease is first identified in Lyme, Connecticut.
- *Saturday Night Live* debuts on NBC.
- Disco is huge.
- Teamster boss Jimmy Hoffa vanishes.
- Philip Morris introduces Miller Lite Beer.

YEAR OF THE CAT 1987

- President Reagan and Soviet Party Secretary Mikhail Gorbachev sign a treaty to reduce the size of both countries' nuclear arsenals.
- The FDA approves the cholesterol-lowering drug Lovastatin.
- Minister Jim Bakker resigns as head of the PTL church after it is revealed that he cheated on his wife Tammy Faye with Jessica Hahn.

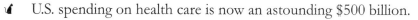

- Ivan Boesky is sentenced to prison and fined $100 million for Wall Street insider trading.
- Microwave oven sales skyrocket and food companies rush to develop microwaveable foods.
- U.S. spending on health care is now an astounding $500 billion.
- Ozone-depleting chlorofluorocarbons are banned at a consortium of nations meeting in Montreal.

YEAR OF THE CAT 1999

- JFK Jr., his wife, and sister-in-law die in a crash in a small plane piloted by John Jr.
- President Clinton is impeached and ultimately acquitted.
- A federal judge rules that Microsoft is a monopoly.
- The Columbine school shooting stuns the nation.
- The world braces for the dreaded Y2K millennium bug; nothing happens.
- Princeton neurobiologist Joseph Tsien creates a smarter mouse by altering a single gene.

337 LIBRARY CATS

Cats everywhere asleep on the shelves like motorized book ends.

—Audrey Thomas

What is a library cat?

The simple answer is "a cat that lives in a library," but there is much more to it than that.

A library cat becomes a member of the community and a beloved member of every library patron's family. Library cats are usually strays that are found wandering around the grounds of a library and are then fed and taken in by the library staff. The cat is then allowed to sleep in the library at night, and it isn't long before the bibliofeline is named and adopted by not only the staff but the patrons and visitors to the library.

Cats and libraries go together very well. The quiet atmosphere, the secluded nooks, the high places, all have great appeal to felines and it is hard to imagine a dog feeling as comfortable or being as "at home" in a library as a cat—especially since dogs sometimes do not like to sit still...well, at least nowhere near as much as cats do. (Maybe this has something to do with the extraordinary number of writers who had and have cats as constant companions?)

The following list was compiled by the indefatigable Gary Roma, who must be the world's authority on this little-known subculture of the feline world. Gary tells me that this list is accurate through February 22, 2001 and that a constantly updated list and map can be found on his Web site at *www.ironfrog.com.*

This list includes the 337 known library cats in the United States. Gary also tells us that there are 222 former residents and 115 current residents (including 9 permanent residents: 6 sculptures, 1 stuffed Siberian tiger, one stuffed mountain lion, and 1 virtual library cat (Michigan's "404," a permanent resident of the Internet Public Library).

Contact info for Gary and his Iron-frog Productions can be found at the end of this chapter.

By the way...there are currently no known library cats in Alaska, Delaware, the District of Columbia, North Carolina, Rhode Island, South Dakota, and Wyoming. It seems to me that residents of these states should try and remedy this travesty as soon as possible, don't you agree?

GARY ROMA/IRON FROG PRODUCTIONS

Melville Dewey of Eastham Public Library, Eastham Mass., keeps watch for overdue books.

ALABAMA

- Dharma
  (Parnell Memorial Library)
- Dr. Seuss (Moundville Elementary School Library)
- Honey Bun (St. Margaret's School Library)
- Tigger (Smiths Station Intermediate School Library)

ALASKA

- There are no known library cats in Alaska.

ARIZONA

- Abigail, Arlo, Cleopatra and Tailer (Cochise County District Library)
- Boots (Benson Public Library)

ARKANSAS

- Angel (Fletcher Branch Library)

CALIFORNIA

- Ack Ack (Inyo County Free Library, Bishop Branch)
- Alis
  (Orange County Public Library)

- Baby
  (Alameda County Main Library)
- Bessie
  (Mechanics' Institute Library)
- Betty Jane, Cream Puff, Feather, Ishi, Jane, Jenny, Sylvia (Aquatic Research Institute Library)
- Booker (Wrightwood Library)
- Chatty Cathy, Elvis, Frank, Grandma, Grayma, Harley, Hughie, Little Bluto, Liz, Malcolm, Martin, Michael Jackson, Nicholson, Newman, Nomo, Ruff, Tom, Tootsie (Simi Valley Library)
- Critter (Crowell Elementary School Library)
- Cynthia (Alameda County Library, Centerville Branch)
- Dewey (Butte County Library, Chico Branch)
- Dewey (Mission Viejo Library)
- Flower Gower Bower Champion (Mill Valley Public Library)
- Flyer (Whittier Public Library)
- Folger
  (Torrance High School Library)
- Gaylord
  (El Centro Public Library)
- Jerry (The College Preparatory School Library)
- K.C. (Kern County Library)
- Kiki (Moorpark Library)
- L.C. (Bonita Vista Middle School Library)

- L.C. (Escondido Public Library)
- L.C. (Santa Cruz Public Library, Boulder Creek Branch)
- Libby (Los Angeles Valley College Library)
- Magnificat (Graduate Theological Union Library)
- Malcolm Forbes and Queen Guinevere (Cumberland Elementary School Library)
- Max (Pasadena Public Library, Hastings Branch)
- McNaughton [aka Mac] (Victorville Library)
- Mildred (University of California Institute of Governmental Studies Library)
- Myrtle and Smokin (Alemany High School Library)
- Pearl Cat [aka P.C.] (San Jose Public Library)
- Petunia (Dublin Library)
- Precious and Theodore Readmore (Bruggemeyer Memorial Library)
- Shava (University of California Long Business and Economics Library)
- Smudge, Sudya, Tigger, Tomas, Tristan (University of California Tomas Rivera Library)
- Sonnet (Torrey Pines High School Library Media Center)
- Winston (South County Library)
- Spookye
  (John Steinbeck Library)

Dewey the cat poses with a few of his favorite books.

COLORADO

- Hemingway (Southern Peaks Public Library)
- Judge Kitty (Fairplay Library)
- L.C. (Central High School Library)
- Libby (Bookcliff Middle School Library)
- Mattie (Bud Werner Memorial Library)
- Samson and Tux (Butch McClanahan Memorial Library)

CONNECTICUT

- Annie and Prudence (James Blackstone Memorial Library)
- Bookums (Windsor Locks Public Library)
- Dewey, Friskie, Junior and Patches (Atwater Memorial Library)
- Emily, John Doe and Melvil Dewey (Mystic and Noank Library)
- Fred (Woodbury Public Library)
- Mitzi Misu (New Haven Free Public Library)
- Ugo (Hotchkiss Library)

DELAWARE

- There are no known library cats in Delaware.

DISTRICT OF COLUMBIA

- There are no known library cats in the District of Columbia.

FLORIDA

- Blackwell (Florida Institute of Technology Evans Library)
- Bookings (Broward County Library)
- Dewey (Martin County Library, Indiantown Branch)
- Legs (Gulliver Preparatory School Library)

GEORGIA

- B.J., Eudora and Woody (Rome-Floyd County Library)
- JamBack (Henry County Library)
- Lady (Ohoopee Regional Library)
- Squeakers (Wesleyan College Willet Memorial Library)
- Tallulah [aka Tally] (Douglas County Library)

HAWAII

- Junior and Gypsy (Kihei Library)

IDAHO

- Archie (Payette Public Library)
- Cali (Culdesac Community Library)
- L.C. Dickens (Garden Valley District Library)

- Laser (Boise Basin Library District)
- The Midnight Cat (Portneuf District Library)

ILLINOIS

- Bookie (Western Illinois Library)
- Puddin' (Chicago Ridge Public Library)
- Simon and Toby (Shapiro Development Center Resident Library)
- Tina (West Chicago Public Library)

INDIANA

- Elizabeth and Roger (Ligonier Public Library)
- Pooh and Tigger (Beech Grove Public Library)

IOWA

- Dewey Readmore Books (Spencer Public Library)
- Gentleman (Scott County Library System)
- Herbie (Herbert Hoover Presidential Library and Museum)

KANSAS

- Casey (Kansas State Hospital Library)
- Libby and The Professor (Haysville Community Library)

- Libby (Girard Public Library)
- Molli Perl Readalot (Hamilton County Library)
- Page (Stevens County Library)
- Sam and Sin Jin [plus two more cats from the 1970's—names unknown] (Osawatomie Public Library)
- Thomas (Johnston Public Library)
- Tiger (Stanton County Library)
- Tommy (Grant County Library)

KENTUCKY

- Browser (Madison County Public Library)
- Dewey Decimal (Campbell County Public Library)
- Smokey Dickens (Bowling Green Public Library)

LOUISIANA

- Davey Crockett [aka Davey Doodle (Lakeshore Branch Library)
- Mandy and Molly (Lilly Thornton Branch Library)

MAINE

- Bam-Bam (Rice Public Library)
- Buffy (Brewer Public Library)
- Eddie and Peaches (Alvan Bolster Ricker Memorial Library)
- Libby and Walker (Walker Memorial Library)

- Mrs. Truman (Abbott Memorial Library)
- Poe and Squiggles (Patten Free Library)

MARYLAND

- There are no known library cats in Maryland.

MASSACHUSETTS

- Booklet Wallenda and Fancy Free (Northborough Free Library)
- Buster (Monson Free Library)
- Charisma and Hec (Boston Public Library, Uphams Corner Branch)
- Dewey (Boston Public Library, Egleston Square Branch)
- Dotty (Centerville Public Library)
- Gordon (Wayland Free Public Library)
- Leo and Leona [lion sculptures] (Boston Public Library)
- Leo Katz (Brockton Public Library)
- Max (Wellfleet Public Library)
- Melville Dewey (Eastham Public Library)
- Molly (Dedham Public Library)
- Pepper (South Hadley Public Library)
- Smoky (Boylston Public Library)
- Spooky (Swansea Public Library)

IRON FROG PRODUCTIONS

Herbie, the library cat of the Herbert Hoover Presidential Library
in West Branch, Iowa, shows off his presidential pad.

MICHIGAN

- 404 [the virtual library cat]
  (Internet Public Library)
- Amelia Bedelia and Pocahantas
  (Ogemaw District Library)
- Booker (Kalkaska County
  Library)
- Charles Dickens (Putnam
  District Library)
- Deuce (Kent District Library)
- Madeline
  (Loutit District Library)
- Rachel
  (Cromaine District Library)
- Tiberius [aka Ty]
  (Cass District Library)
- Whisper (Sturgis Public Library)
- [Name unknown]
  (Romeo District Library)

MINNESOTA

- O'Keefe (Duluth Public Library)
- Pirate, Sinclair and Sophie
  (Minneapolis Public Library,
  Walker Branch)
- Reggie and Sadie
  (Bryant Library)
- The Library Cat [sculpture]
  (Detroit Lakes Public Library)

MISSISSIPPI

- Dewey Decimal and Powell Ricks (Ricks Memorial Library)
- Fisk (Judge George W. Armstrong Library)
- Miss Gussie and Miss Theo (Evans Memorial Library)
- Tigger (Ocean Springs Municipal Library)

MISSOURI

- Emerson Booker (Gentry County Library)
- Woody (St. Louis Community College Meramec Library)

MONTANA

- L.C. (Flathead County Library)
- Maizie (Glasgow City/County Library)
- Paul (Paul M. Adams Memorial Library)

NEBRASKA

- Goldie (Broken Bow Public Library)

NEVADA

- Baker and Taylor (Douglas County Public Library)
- Dewey (Elko County Library)
- Buddha (University of Nevada Lied Library) [Former resident]

NEW HAMPSHIRE

- Carnegie (Rochester Public Library)
- Elliot (Manchester City Library)
- Fiskers and Rosy O'Grady (Fiske Free Library)

NEW JERSEY

- Dewey (Westwood Public Library)
- Dewey, Gimpy Cat and Queen (Hunterdon County Library)
- Oscar (Rivervale Free Public Library)

NEW MEXICO

- Ed (Farmington Public Library)
- Socks (Clovis-Carver Public Library)

NEW YORK

- Agatha (Morrisville Library)
- Blackie (Poestenkill Library)
- Bookend (Jervis Public Library)
- Catalog (Community Free Library)
- Deml (Edward and Doris Mortola Library)
- Dewey Decimal, Jesse and Kitty (Cazenovia Public Library)
- Fluffy and Shitara (Sullivan Free Library)

IRON FROG PRODUCTIONS

Dr. Seuss of the Bradford Area Public Library in Bradford, Penn., poses as the "Cat in the Bag."

- Fortitude and Patience [lion sculptures] (New York Public Library)
- George (Tompkins County Public Library)
- Hilfrel (Highland Free Library)
- Kitch (LaSalle Library)
- Morris [stuffed Siberian tiger] (State University of New York Morrisville College Library)
- Muffin (Putnam Valley Free Library)
- Orphan Annie Raims (Ontario County Records and Archives Center)
- Pippin and Watson (Earlville Free Library)
- Potter (Brooklyn Public Library, Sheepshead Bay Branch)
- Stax (Lee-Whedon Memorial Library)
- Tico (Onondaga Public Library, Hazard Branch)
- Toner (New Woodstock Free Library)

NORTH CAROLINA

- There are no known library cats in North Carolina.

NOTH DAKOTA

- Cleo Boom Boom Marie (Fargo Public Library)

OHIO

- Alex (Brecksville Public Library)

- Barney and Dewey (Hudson Library and Historical Society)
- Buddy (Green County Public Library Service Center)
- Dewey (Tipp City Public Library)
- Emily and William Shakespeare [aka Willy] (Wickliffe Public Library)
- Groucho, Miss Drew Kitty, Morrie Carnegie, Runt, Tigger, Tuxedo One and Tuxedo Two (Paulding County Carnegie Library)
- Jiggers (Westlake Porter Public Library)
- Lucy and Ricky (Lepper Library)
- Ms. Kitty (Lane Public Library)
- Smoke (Columbus Metropolitan Library, Franklinton Branch)
- Sophie (Highland County District Library)

OKLAHOMA

- Austen and Jane (Herbert F. Tyler Memorial Library)

OREGON

- Agatha Christie (Driftwood Library)

BEA CRAIG/IRON FROG PRODUCTIONS

Carnegie, of the Rochester Public Library, Rochester, N.Y., looks up "dinner" in the card catalog.

- Agnes (Tillamook County Library)
- Benjamin Franklin, Marion, Turtle (Newport Public Library)
- Boris (Klamath Library)
- Cat and the Fiddle [sculpture] (Eugene Public Library)
- Catalog (Jackson County Public Library System)
- Dewey (North Salem High School Library)
- Huggins (Hood River County Library)

- Libby
  (Creswell High School Library)
- Libby (Tigard Public Library)
- Milkshake (View Acres
  School Library)
- Page (Gladstone Public Library)
- Pee-Wee and Snooter
  (Willamette University Library)
- Smokey (Rogue Community
  College Library)
- Stacks (Estacada Public Library)

PENNSYLVANIA

- Dr. Seuss
  (Bradford Area Public Library)
- Mr. Kitty (Montgomery Area
  Public Library)
- Mrs. Murphy
  (Plymouth Public Library)
- Sheba
  (Stey-Nevant Public Library)
- The Nittany Lion [stuffed
  mountain lion] (Penn State
  University Pattee Library)

RHODE ISLAND

- There are no known library cats
  in Rhode Island.

SOUTH CAROLINA

- Topaz (Oakland Elementary
  School Library)
- Webster (University of South
  Carolina Library)

SOUTH DAKOTA

- There are no known library cats
  in South Dakota.

TENNESSEE

- Bailey
  (The Ensworth School Library)

TEXAS

- B.T. and Gabby
  (Temple Public Library)
- Booker
  (R.J. Kleberg Public Library)
- Cleo and Willa (Mineola
  Memorial Public Library)
- Deci and Dewey (Fort Worth
  Public Library)
- Molli (Azle Public Library)
- Monty (Montgomery
  Elementary School Library)
- Simba (Terrell Public Library)
- Spinny (Beaumont Public Library
  System, Spindletop Branch)

UTAH

- Libby (College of
  Eastern Utah Library)

VERMONT

- Pages
  (Brandon Free Public Library)

VIRGINIA

- Dewey (Central Rappahannock
  Regional Library)

- Molly Van Wyck (Norfolk Public Library, Van Wyck Branch)
- Dewey (Bellwood Elementary School Library)

WASHINGTON

- Banjo (Wenatchee Valley College Library)
- Bingo, Chancey, Pippi Longstocking, Rosebud, Libby (Meeker Middle School Library)
- Booker (Seattle Public Library, Rainier Beach Branch)
- Co-Co, Emma, William (Delta Society Resource Center Library)
- Dui (Kitsap Regional Library)
- L.C. and L.C.[II] (Ephrata Public Library)
- Max, Raymond (Port Townsend Public Library)
- Momcat (King County Library System, White Center Branch)
- P.C., Rubio, Sam Hill (Timberland North Mason Library)
- Scully (Central Elementary School Library)

- Spike, Tiger (Lake Forest Park Elementary School Library)
- Teva (Anacortes Public Library)
- Tigger (King County Public Library, Tukwila Branch)
- Trixie (Ocean Shores Public Library)
- Willoughby (John Campbell School Library)

WEST VIRGINIA

- Dewey Decimal [aka D.D.] (Princeton Public Library)
- Ms. Dewey (Fairview Public Library)

WISCONSIN

- Cleopatra and Webster (Mead Public Library)
- Kinky (Kilbourn Public Library)
- Maggie (Salem Community Library)

WYOMING

- There are no known library cats in Wyoming.

"PUSS IN BOOKS"

Puss in Books is a documentary about library cats, and one of the reasons it is a remarkable film is because director Gary Roma does not pussyfoot around (sorry) when it comes to giving the anti-library cat faction their chance to speak. Admittedly, the anti-cat people (most of whom claim allergies as the reason cats should not be allowed to live in libraries) come off as somewhat curmudgeonly and the overall impression one comes away with from this documentary is that library cats enhance a patron's visit to the library, much the way a cat in a house enhances the residence. (And the tape is worth owning just for the poignant story of Baker and Taylor—two cats from the Douglas County Public Library in Nevada named for the giant book distribution company.)

Gary Roma's "Library Cats" documentary *Puss in Books* is available for purchase from Iron Frog Productions, 31 Worcester Street, Boston, MA 02118-3398. The cost is $19.95 for individuals and $24.95 for libraries. (Please add $3.00 for shipping and handling.) An order form is available at *www.ironfrog.com*. For more information, call (888) 208-0331 or send an email to roma@ironfrog.com.

Gary Roma/Iron Frog Productions

31 Worcester Street

Boston, MA 02118-3398

(888) 208-0331

roma@ironfrog.com

www.ironfrog.com

For even more information about the entire library cats gestalt, you can also contact:

The Library Cat Society

Phyllis Lahti

Box 274

Moorhead, MN 56561-0274

For info on other establishments where cats take up residence, check out...

1. *Cathedral Cats* by Richard Surman, published by HarperCollinsReligious. It documents the many cats that live in and on the grounds of cathedrals in Great Britain.

2. *Cats at Work* by Rhonda Gray and Stephen T. Robinson, published by Abbeville Press. It includes photos of cats working at a bird store, the Humane Society of New York, a hair stylist's studio, a lingerie store, the New York Shakespeare Festival costume shop, a hat factory, a cat specialty store, a dance studio, a radio station, a record store, a billiards hall, a pinball machine dealer, a deli, a bakery, a wine store, a pharmacy, a laundromat, a public relations firm, a movie theater, bookstores, a detective's office in the New York Police Department, a fire station, and many other locations across the United States.

FACTS ABOUT "CATS": THE MUSICAL

This feature is included in *The Cat Book of Lists* because T.S. Eliot was a cat lover and his "cat" poems are the source for what may ultimately turn out to be the most popular musical in the history of musical theater.

20 CATS FACTS

- The musical *Cats* is based on T.S. Eliot's book of poems *Old Possum's Book of Practical Cats*.
- T.S. Eliot's widow, Valerie Eliot gave Andrew Lloyd Weber an unpublished 8-line fragment about Grizabella the Glamour Cat, that Eliot had left out of his book because he felt it was too depressing for children.
- T.S. Eliot once turned down a request from Walt Disney to use his Practical Cats poems in an animated feature. Eliot explained that his cats "were hard-scrabble alley cats, not cute little anthropomorphs."
- The first time *Cats* director Trevor Nunn heard the song "Memory," he said, "What is the date? What is the hour? Because you have just heard a smash hit by Lloyd Webber."
- "Memory" has been recorded by over 150 artists, from Barbra Streisand and Johnny Mathis, to Liberace. Barry Manilow's rendition was a top-40 hit in the United States.
- The original production of *Cats* opened at the New London Theatre, in the West End on May 11, 1981.

- In 1989, the British production of *Cats* celebrated its 3,358th performance, making it the longest-running musical in the history of British musical theater.

- On January 29, 1996 the London production of *Cats* celebrated its 6,141st performance and became the longest-running musical in the history of West End theatre.

- In April 1999 the gross box office for the London production of *Cats* topped $184 million.

- *Cats* opened in the United States on Broadway at the Winter Garden Theatre on October 7, 1982, and played continuously until September 10, 2000 for a total of 7,485 performances.

- In September 2000, the gross box office for the American production of *Cats* topped $400 million.

- *Cats* motto was "Now and Forever."

- The original Broadway cast recording of *Cats* sold more than 2 million copies.

- On June 19, 1997, *Cats* became the longest-running musical in the history of Broadway musical theater.

- Since it opened, *Cats* has been presented in 26 countries and more than 300 cities.

- *Cats* has been translated into 10 languages: Japanese, German, Hungarian, Norwegian, Finnish, Dutch, Swedish, French, Spanish and Italian.

- The title of the show has never been translated into a foreign language.

- The elaborate makeup for each character took between 30 minutes and an hour to apply.

- 59,705 condoms were used to protect the singers' body microphones from perspiration and make-up.

- During its Broadway run, Winter Garden workers removed a total of 237 pounds of gum from under the theater's seats.

ANDREW LLOYD WEBER'S SYNOPSIS OF "CATS"

A complete synopsis of the play is available on the Andrew Lloyd Weber Web site *reallyuseful.com* and is the production's official summary of the musical for the media and fans.

THE 30 CATS IN "CATS"

- Grizabella the Glamour Cat
- Gus the Theatre Cat
- Old Deuteronomy
- Bombalurina
- Munkustrap
- Rum Tum Tugger
- Demeter
- Skimbleshanks the Railway Cat
- Bustopher Jones
- Rumpleteazer
- Mungojerrie
- Jennyanydots the Gumbie Cat
- Magical Mr. Mistoffelees
- Jellylorum
- Victoria
- Plato
- Macavity the Mystery Cat
- Jemima
- Coricopat
- Tantomile
- Pouncival
- Electra
- Etcetera
- Tumblebrutus
- Asparagus
- Alonzo
- Exotica
- Admetus
- Rumpus Cat
- Cassandra

17 AWARDS FOR "CATS"

LONDON PRODUCTION

1981 Laurence Olivier Awards

- Musical of the Year
- Outstanding Achievement of the Year in Musicals: Gillian Lynne

1981 Evening Standard Award

- Best Musical

AMERICAN PRODUCTION

1983 Tony Awards

- Best Musical
- Best Book
- Best Score
- Best Director: Trevor Nunn
- Best Supporting Musical Actress: Betty Buckley
- Best Costumes: John Napier
- Best Lighting: David Hersey

1983 Drama Desk Awards

- Best Music
- Best Costumes
- Best Lighting

Grammy

- Best Show Album

New York Outer Critics' Circle Award

- Best Musical

FRANCE

Moliere Award

- Best Musical

CANADA

Dora Mavor Moore Award

- Best Musical

A CABINET OF WHITE HOUSE CATS

Artists like cats; soldiers like dogs.
—Desmond Morris

United States presidents are just like regular folk...er, almost. Many Chief Execs had beloved companion animals before ascending to the highest office in the world, and after becoming president, many brought their pets with them to Washington.

There have been more presidential dogs than cats, but we won't talk about that. (To give presidential dog owners their due, though, many also had cats.)

Over the years, the White House has taken on the nature of a zoo (and I'll leave it to you to find the many meanings in that innocent remark), never more so than when Teddy Roosevelt occupied that hallowed home.

Here is a look at America's First Felines, from Lincoln to Bush (the second one).

ABRAHAM LINCOLN (16TH PRESIDENT)

Tabby. This feline holds the distinction of being the very first White House cat.

Three unnamed cats. These White House felines followed Tabby.

RUTHERFORD HAYES (19TH PRESIDENT)

Siam. This was a Siamese cat presented to President Hayes and was the first of its breed to come to the United States.

THEODORE ROOSEVELT (26TH PRESIDENT)

Slippers and Tom Quartz. These 2 kitties were part of a Teddy Roosevelt White House menagerie that included 5 dogs, 5 bears,

5 guinea pigs, 2 kangaroo rats, assorted lizards, several roosters, an owl, a badger, a pony, a macaw, a flying squirrel, a raccoon, a coyote, a lion, a hyena, a piebald (spotted) rat, several snakes, 12 horses, and, for good measure, a zebra.

WOODROW WILSON (28TH PRESIDENT)

Several unnamed cats.

CALVIN COOLIDGE (29TH PRESIDENT)

Bounder, Smokey, and Tiger. These were ordinary domestic housecats. It isn't known how they felt about sharing quarters with Blackey.

Blackey. This was, no joke, a bobcat.

JOHN KENNEDY (35TH PRESIDENT)

Tom Kitten, aka Tom Terrific. Tom was one of several pets the Kennedy children had when their father was in the White House, including a beer-drinking rabbit and a cobra.

GERALD FORD (38TH PRESIDENT)

Shan, aka Chan. This was a Siamese who shared the White House with a Golden Retriever.

JIMMY CARTER (39TH PRESIDENT)

Misty Malarky Ying Yang. Misty belonged to Amy Carter and holds the record for longest name of any White House cat.

RONALD REAGAN (40TH PRESIDENT)

Several unnamed cats.

BILL CLINTON (42ND PRESIDENT)

Socks. Socks didn't get along with Buddy, President Clinton's Labrador retriever, and when Clinton left office in 2001, Socks was adopted by Clinton's secretary, Betty Currie.

GEORGE W. BUSH (43RD PRESIDENT)

India. This well-behaved, declawed black cat moved to Washington from Texas after Bush won the controversial Presidential election of 2001. India's feline cohort Ernie remained in Texas. He did not like the White House or Washington.

26 THINGS CATS SYMBOLIZE

"Symbols often take the form of words, visual images, or gestures that are used to convey ideas and beliefs. All human cultures use symbols to express the underlying structure of their social systems, to represent ideal cultural characteristics, such as beauty, and to ensure that the culture is passed on to new generations. Symbolic relationships are learned rather than biologically or naturally determined, and each culture has its own symbols."

—*The Dictionary of Cultural Literacy*

Bet you can't find this many esoteric symbols for dogs...not that there's anything wrong with that!

- Corn
- Craftiness
- Demons
- Divination
- Evil
- The female species
- Female sexuality
- Fertility
- Grain
- Love
- Magic
- The male phallus
- Marriage

- The moon
- Mystery
- The occult
- Psychic ability
- Satan
- Serpents
- The sun
- Vampires
- Venus
- The Virgin Mary
- Vision
- The weather
- Witches

TO DREAM OF A CAT

10,000 *Dreams Interpreted* by Gustavus Hindman Miller was first published in 1903, revised in 1931, and to this day is still considered one of the most comprehensive "dreams" books ever written. In this fascinating excerpt, Miller analyzes exactly what he thinks dreams of cats, kittens, leopards, lions, lynxes, panther, tails, and tigers may mean. You may not agree with some of these interpretations, but they do paint an intriguing picture of how cats were perceived as symbols and what those symbols signified for "dreamers" at the beginning of the 20th Century. Personally, I consider these interpretations to be overwhelmingly negative regarding the meaning of a feline in a dream. I think this may be a holdover from the days in which a cat was believed to be a magickal creature with powers that could be dangerous. The perception of cats today has changed, but these dream analyses do provide an amazing snapshot of the super-stitions associated with cats in 1900.

DREAMS OF A CAT

- To dream of a cat, denotes ill luck, if you do not succeed in killing it or driving it from your sight. If the cat attacks you, you will have enemies who will go to any extreme to blacken your reputation and to cause you loss of property. But if you succeed in banishing it, you will overcome great obstacles and rise in fortune and fame.

- If you meet a thin, mean, and dirty-looking cat, you will have bad news from the absent. Some friend lies at death's door; but if you chase it out of sight, your friend will recover after a long and lingering sickness.

197

Emma and Abby settling down for a cat nap.

- To hear the scream or the mewing of a cat, some false friend is using all the words and work at his command to do you harm.

- To dream that a cat scratches you, an enemy will succeed in wrenching from you the profits of a deal that you have spent many days making.

- If a young woman dreams that she is holding a cat or kitten, she will be influenced into some impropriety through the treachery of others.

- To dream of a clean white cat, denotes entanglements which, while seemingly harmless, will prove a source of sorrow and loss of wealth.

- When a merchant dreams of a cat, he should put his best energies to work, as his competitors are about to succeed in demolishing his standard of dealing, and he will be forced to other measures if he undersells others and still succeeds.

- To dream of seeing a cat and snake on friendly terms signifies the beginning of an angry struggle. It denotes that an enemy is being entertained by you with the intention of using him to find out some secret which you believe concerns yourself; uneasy of his confidences given, you will endeavor to disclaim all knowledge of his actions, as you are fearful that things divulged, concerning your private life, may become public.

- To dream that a dog kills a cat in your presence, is significant of profitable dealings and some unexpected pleasure.
- If a young woman sees a cat in her lap, she will be endangered by a seductive enemy.

DREAMS OF A KITTEN

- For a woman to dream of a beautiful fat, white kitten, omens artful deception will be practised upon her, which will almost ensnare her to destruction, but her good sense and judgment will prevail in warding off unfortunate complications. If the kittens are soiled, or colored and lean, she will be victimized into glaring indiscretions.
- To dream of kittens denotes abominable small troubles and vexations will pursue...you, unless you kill the kitten, and then you will overcome these worries.
- To see snakes kill kittens, you have enemies who in seeking to injure you will work harm to themselves.

DREAMS OF A LEOPARD

- To dream of a leopard attacking you, denotes that while the future seemingly promises fair, success holds many difficulties through misplaced confidence.
- To kill one, intimates victory in your affairs.
- To see one caged, denotes that enemies will surround but fail to injure you.
- To see leopards in their native place trying to escape from you, denotes that you will be embarrassed in business or love, but by persistent efforts you will overcome difficulties.
- To dream of a leopard's skin, denotes that your interests will be endangered by a dishonest person who will win your esteem.

DREAMS OF A LION

- To dream of a lion, signifies that a great force is driving you.
- If you subdue the lion, you will be victorious in any engagement.
- If it overpowers you, then you will be open to the successful attacks of enemies.

- To see caged lions, denotes that your success depends upon your ability to cope with opposition.

- To see a man controlling a lion in its cage, or out denotes success in business and great mental power. You will be favorably regarded by women.

- To see young lions, denotes new enterprises, which will bring success if properly attended.

- For a young woman to dream of young lions, denotes new and fascinating lovers.

- For a woman to dream that she sees Daniel in the lions' den, signifies that by her intellectual qualifications and personal magnetism, she will win fortune and lovers to her highest desire.

- To hear the roar of a lion, signifies unexpected advancement and preferment with women.

- To see a lion's head over you, showing his teeth by snarls, you are threatened with defeat in your upward rise to power.

- To see a lion's skin, denotes a rise to fortune and happiness.

- To ride one, denotes courage and persistency in surmounting difficulties.

- To dream you are defending your children from a lion with a pen-knife, foretells enemies will threaten to overpower you, and will well nigh succeed if you allow any artfulness to persuade you for a moment from duty and business obligations.

DREAMS OF A LYNX

- To dream of seeing a lynx, enemies are undermining your business and disrupting your home affairs. For a woman, this dream indicates that she has a wary woman rivaling her in the affections of her lover. If she kills the lynx, she will overcome her rival.

DREAMS OF A PANTHER

- To see a panther and experience fright, denotes that contracts in love or business may be canceled unexpectedly, owing to adverse influences working against your honor. But killing, or over-powering it, you will experience joy and be successful in your undertakings. Your surroundings will take on fair prospects.

- If one menaces you by its presence, you will have disappointments in business. Other people will likely recede from their promises to you.

- If you hear the voice of a panther, and experience terror or fright, you will have unfavorable news, coming in the way of reducing profit or gain, and you may have social discord; no fright forebodes less evil.

DREAMS OF A TAIL

- To dream of seeing only the tail of a beast, unusual annoyance is indicated where pleasures seemed assured.
- To cut off the tail of an animal, denotes that you will suffer misfortune by your own carelessness.
- To dream that you have the tail of a beast grown on you, denotes that your evil ways will cause you untold distress, and strange events will cause you perplexity.

DREAMS OF A TIGER

- To dream of a tiger advancing towards you, you will be tormented and persecuted by enemies. If it attacks you, failure will bury you in gloom. If you succeed in warding it off, or killing it, you will be extremely successful in all your undertakings.
- To see one running away from you, is a sign that you will overcome opposition, and rise to high positions.
- To see them in cages, foretells that you will foil your adversaries.
- To see rugs of tiger skins, denotes that you are on the way to enjoy luxurious ease and pleasure.

FAMOUS CAT OWNERS

*"As every cat owner knows,
nobody owns a cat."*

—Ellen Perry Berkeley

This is a list of some of the famous people, past and present, (followed by the name of their pets), who manifested incredible taste when it came to choosing their companion animals.

- Muhammad Ali (retired boxing legend): Icarus
- Joan Baez (singer/songwriter): Carlangas
- Daniel Boone (frontiersman): Bluegrass
- Carol Burnett (comedienne, actress): Roxy
- Roger Caras (animal expert): Eartha Cat
- Raymond Chandler (writer): Taki
- Winston Churchill (leader): Jock
- Colette (writer): La Chat Dernier
- Carol Connors (singer): Minstrel (aka, Major); Music Man (aka MandM, aka Minor)
- Jimmy Connors (tennis star): Kismet
- Drea DeMatteo (actress, *The Sopranos*): Treble; Bass
- Cameron Diaz (actress): Little Man
- Jaime Nicole Dudney (actress, Barbara Mandrell's daughter): Isabella
- Kirsten Dunst (actress): Tasmania (aka Taz)
- Michael Feinstein (singer): Bing Clawsby
- Eva Gabor (actress): Zsa Zsa
- Leeza Gibbons (talk-show host): Alex
- Robert Goulet (singer): Vincent; Wart

- Matt Groening (writer/cartoonist): Frosty
- Buddy Hackett (comedian): Charlie; Sgt. Maguire; Muffin
- Victor Hugo (writer): Chanoine; Gavroche
- Shawnae Jebbia (Miss USA 1998): Meatball
- Samuel Johnson (writer): Hodge
- Swoosie Kurtz (actress): Baby Rose
- Pope Leo XII (Pontiff): Micetto
- Barbara Mandrell (Country singer/songwriter): Peaches; Love; Tink; Vanderbilt; Kumate
- Joe Mantegna (actor): Rosie O' Kitty
- Mohammed (religious leader): Muezza
- Joe Namath (retired football legend): Poppet
- Graham Nash (singer/songwriter): Frogurt
- Julie Newmar (actress): Bird
- Nick Nolte (actor): Kitty
- Greg Norman (pro golfer): Telegram Sam
- Gary Oldman (actor): Soymilk (aka Mook)
- Edgar Allan Poe (writer): Catarina
- Kevin Richardson (actor): Quincy
- Albert Schweitzer (theologian and physician): Sizi
- Melody Thomas Scott (actress): Killer
- Sir Walter Scott (writer): Hinse
- Liz Smith (writer): Mr. Sotto Voce
- Jil St. John (actress): Sunny
- Martha Stewart (style and etiquette maven): Teeny; Weeny; Mozart; Beethoven; Verdi; Vivaldi; Berlioz; Bartok
- Sally Struthers (actress): Joan Pawford, Kitty Dearest
- Tiffani-Amber Thiessen (actress): Sadie
- Alex Trebek (*Jeopardy* host): Linger Dinger
- Mark Twain (writer): Blatherskite; Sour Mash; Stray Kit; Sin; Satan
- Kelly Van Halen (actress): Clack
- Kurt Vonnegut, Jr. (writer): Claude
- Robert Wagner (actor): Pepe
- H.G. Wells (writer): Mr. Peter Wells

OTHER FAMOUS CAT LOVERS...

Petrarch, Ernest Hemingway, Florence Nightingale, Cardinal Richelieu, St. Agatha, St. Francis of Assisi, St. Gregory the Great, St. Ives, St. Jerome, St. Molig, Jeremy Bentham, Colette, Montaigne, Horace Walpole, and Abraham Lincoln.

SIEGFRIED AND ROY'S 38 KITTIES

Siegfried and Roy have staged a spectacular live animal act in Las Vegas for decades and they would probably be the first to admit that their incredible lions and tigers are the real stars of the show. Here is a list of the 38 big cats owned by Siegfried and Roy, all of whom appear in their stage show.

- **The Royal White Tigers of Nevada Sitarra:** Akbar-Kabul, Mirage, Mantra, Johan, Neva, Shasadee, Nevada, Sieg-Roy, Vegas, Christmas, Nickolei, Noele, Fuji, Tokyo, Osaka, Red, White, Blue, Samsara, Mahatma, Orissa, Mantacore, and She-Ra.
- **The White Lions of Timbavati Sarmoti:** Shaka, Secret, Mystery, Hope, Pride, Joy, Destiny, Vision, Quest, Passion, Prosperity, Future, and Sunshine.

FAMOUS CAT HATERS

Boo! Hiss!

Desmond Morris's observation that "Artists like cats; soldiers like dogs" is dramatically illustrated by this list of avowed cat haters. Most of these guys are military leaders and conquerors, with a few despots thrown in for bad measure.

Brahms, Howard, and Webster are a surprise, though.

- Alexander the Great—A conqueror who reportedly wept when he realized he had no more "worlds to conquer."
- Napoleon Bonaparte—A short, squat man with delusions of grandeur and an over-reaching military.
- Johannes Brahms—A brilliant composer of beautiful music; liked to shoot cats with a bow and arrow.
- Julius Caesar—First Century B.C. Roman dictator.
- Dwight D. Eisenhower—Invaded Normandy, overthrew the Nazis, U.S. President.
- Henry III—16th Century King; hated Protestants.
- Adolf Hitler—No comment.
- Robert E. Howard—Writer, creator of Conan the Barbarian.
- Genghis Khan—Astonishingly cruel 12th century Mongolian emperor.
- Benito Mussolini—Italian dictator, big fan of Fascism.
- Noah Webster—Created the seminal English dictionary.

21 HORROR AND SCIENCE FICTION SHORT STORIES ABOUT CATS

16 ANIMATED FAMILY MOVIES ABOUT CATS

Thee movies should all be available on video and are still fun for kids of all ages, even though some of these are over 40 years old.

- *Hyde and Go Tweet* (1960): The wacky adventures of Sylvester the Cat and Tweety Bird.
- *Mouse and Garden* (1960): The wacky adventures of Sylvester the Cat and his feline friend Sam.
- *Who Scent You?* (1960): Pepe Le Pew the skunk pursues a black cat he thinks is a skunk.
- *A—Scent of the Matterhorn* (1961): Pepe Le Pew the skunk pursues a black cat he thinks is a skunk. (Yup.)
- *Birds of a Father* (1961): Sylvester discovers that his son Junior is best friends with a bird!
- *Calypso Cat* (1962): Tom Cat stows away on a cruise ship to pursue a cat he is smitten with.
- *Fish and Slips* (1962): Sylvester takes Junior on a fishing trip—in an aquarium!
- *The Jet Cage* (1962): Sylvester pursues Tweety—who is flying around in a jet-powered birdcage!
- *Louvre Come Back to Me!* (1962): Pepe Le Pew the skunk pursues a black cat he thinks is a skunk. (Yup, again.)
- *Mouse Into Space* (1962): Jerry decides to travel to outer space because there are no cats there, but Tom stows away on the rocket.

- *Claws in the Lease* (1963): Sylvester tries to sneak into a house where his son Junior is living after Junior was adopted by a woman who only wanted a kitten.

- *An American Tail* (1986): Fievel, a Russian mouse, travels to America because he has heard it is a wondrous place where there are no cats. He is in for a surprise.

- *Daffy Duck's Quackbusters* (1988): In an attempt to keep a multimillion dollar inheritance, Daffy Duck opens a "ghostbusting" service, and hires all his friends, including Bugs Bunny, Porky Pig, and Sylvester Cat

- *An American Tail: Fievel Goes West* (1991): The Mousekewitzes (great name, eh?) travel West where they have heard that cats and mice live in peace. And, once again, overly optimistic mice are in for a surprise.

- *Tom and Jerry: The Movie* (1992): Tom and Jerry attempt to help a little girl who is trying to get away from her cruel guardian.

- *Cats Don't Dance* (1997): Danny the cat travels to Hollywood with the dream of becoming a movie star—not knowing that animals are only used as extras in the movies.

CATS IN CYBERSPACE

The Internet is cat friendly. There are literally millions of Web sites with cat relevant info, and there are cat newsgroups, cat chat rooms, cat clubs, and cat photo archives galore on the Web. A recent search for "cats" on a few popular search engines returned 1,520,000 hits from Google; 1,933,805 hits from Excite; and a whopping 4,344,650 hits from Northern Light. If you're interested in chatting with fellow feline fanciers, you can check out the newsgroups *alt.cats*, *alt.animals.felines*, *rec.pets.cats*, *rec.pets.cats-health+behavior*, and *rec.pets.cats.misc*. You can also visit the Web sites of the major cat food manufacturers, many of which are full of useful and fun information, the opportunity to subscribe to mailing lists, and free offers.

ANIMAL PLANET SERIES THAT FEATURE CATS

Do you have cable or satellite TV? And if not, do you have a hospitable neighbor with either?

Animal Planet is a cable channel that is offered as part of a basic cable subscription package on a great many cable systems (Comcast, TCI, Cablevision, and the like) all over the country, as well as via Satellite.

Animal Planet offers a wide variety of animal programming, ranging from wildlife shows to shows on pet care. Here is a list of the Animal Planet series that regularly air features about cats:

- *Amazing Animal Videos*
- *Big Cat Diary*
- *Emergency Vets*
- *Pet Story*
- *Planet's Funniest Animals*

Animal Planet also has a terrific Web presence at their Web site *AnimalPlanet.com*. It is a fun site which offers information about all kinds of animals for adults and kids, plus show listings, a search engine, and a variety of animal-specific links.

10 UNIQUE CAT PRODUCTS AND SERVICES

These 10 products and services suggest that we cat lovers might be just a tad obsessed with out pets. Not that there's anything wrong with that, either.

THE LAP CAT BED

PetLap makes a cat bed that looks and feels like a real lap. It looks like a pair of denim shorts stuffed with soft padding so that "Your cat can still have a lap to sit in even when yours is not available."

PetLap Company
3108 Finch St.
Davis, CA 95616
(530) 758-2707
sales@petlap.com
www.petlap.com

CAT PSYCHICS

These folks will tell you what your cat is thinking...for a fee, of course.

The Psychic Source
1-877-468-8587

CAT CHAT LINES

Talk to live "Cat Chatters" from all over the United States...for a fee, of course. (Although they state in their ad that "Profits will go to help homeless Southern Californian Cats.")

1-800-382-6757

GREETING CARDS FOR CATS

They have catnip in them, which the company says makes the cats want to "open" the cards themselves.

(800) 390-5588 or (304) 466-1437

www.mtlioncatnip.com

KITTY SHOW VIDEO TOY

This is a video that presents a 2-hour show of bugs trapped inside your television. The company says the video is enhanced for "Cat Vision."

(615) 904-8716

www.kittyshow.com

FREEZE-DRY PRESERVATION OF CATS

From the company's Web site:

"Today's technology has made freeze-dry preservation—a more comforting alternative—an option. With this method we can preserve your pet in a restful and peaceful manner. Although they are no longer living, we can keep them in our presence. A pet is many things to different people. To many pet owners burial and cremation are not acceptable. Very often we receive calls from grieving pet owners, and many of them tell us "we just cannot stand the thought of burying our pet." If your pet has passed on to the "Rainbow Bridge" or you are making preparations for the loss of your pet, you may want to consider our service. If you think Freeze-dry preservation might be an alternative to burial or cremation, please give us a call. You will be treated with respect and dignity by our staff during this difficult time. We are the largest Freeze-dry service in North America and have been serving pet owners since 1989."

STACEY A. FARKAS

Buttons: feline carpenter.

Eddy Enterprises
315 N. Main St.
Slater, MO 65349
(800) 529-3470
www.pet-animalpreservation.com

PERSONALIZED CAT PLACEMATS

You can order placemats with your cat's picture and name on it. They are suitable for either a human's table or a cat's (i.e., the floor).

www.pet-placemats.com

CAT OUTFITS

Now you can buy a wardrobe for your cat. This company offers cat outfits, including tuxedos, cowboy outfits, police uniforms, dresses, hats, and more. If, for some reason, you have the desire to dress up your cat, here's your chance.

Cat-Catron Fashions
400 South St.
Apartment 28
Ft. Bragg, CA 95437
(707) 962-0725
www.catronfashion.com

CAT "TOY OF THE MONTH"

Subscribe your kitty to this service and she will receive a brand-new toy every month, personally addressed to her, that she can play with for four minutes, swat it under the refrigerator, and then ignore for the rest of the month.

Cat Toy of the Month
P.O. Box 5700
Sherman Oaks, CA 91413
(818) 782-9343
www.cattoyofthemonth.com

CAT PHOTO LICENSE PLATES

You can now tell the world (or at least people behind you in traffic) just how much you love your cat by having his picture emblazoned on your car's license plate. (Wonder how the state motor vehicle departments feel about this?)

Picture Your Plates
(902) 462-3889
www.pictureyourlicenseplates.com

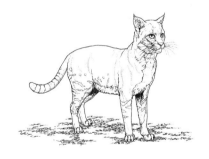

5 REALLY CHEAP CAT TOYS

And we'll have fun, fun, fun...

We've all heard the complaints of parents who buy their toddlers amazingly expensive and educational toys (like building sets, miniature kitchens, or toy musical instruments) and the kids play with the toys for a few minutes and then spend hours playing with the box the toys came in, right? This happens with cats, too. So to outsmart your kitty (who would undoubtedly prefer to play with the package the $10 activity wheel came in rather than the $10 activity wheel), here are five toys guaranteed to provide hours of amusement for your fickle kitty, and yet not cost you a dime.

1. A CRUMPLED PIECE OF PAPER

Discovering just how much fun cats can have with a crumpled piece of paper was a revelation to me. As is often the case, my cat taught me that what I thought was trash was actually a plaything of great importance.

I had made a couple of notes on a white scratch pad, the ones that are 3" x 5", and I decided to throw the sheet away. I ripped the page off the pad, crumpled it up, and threw it in the trash basket. Bennie saw me throw it, and ran to my office pail, almost arriving in time to catch the wadded up piece of paper in mid-air. What he did do was grab it out of the pail (it was on top of a bunch of other papers) and immediately begin batting it around the floor. A crumpled up piece of scrap paper is light enough so that, like the best cat toys, it seems to take on a life of its own. After hitting it around for a while, he then picked it up in his mouth and began chewing it, liking the feeling of the paper ball's edges stimulating his scent glands situated on the side of his mouth.

This chewing is the final stage of the toy's life.

After a couple of minutes of mastication, the ball is no longer even a semblance of round and, instead, is a flattened, soggy piece of white mush. But that's OK, because scrap paper is cheap enough so that you can give him another one anytime you feel like it.

Some recommendations: anything bigger than the aforementioned 3" by 5" size paper will crumple into a ball too big to really play with. Also, use only white paper, since your cat will undoubtedly chew it and you don't want him swallowing colored dyes from the paper. Also, use a blank piece of paper. If you write on it, he may then end up getting some of the ink in his mouth when he wets the paper.

One caution about this toy, though. Your cat will become conditioned to think that every time you tear off a sheet of scrap paper, he will be getting a new toy. Since I'm a full-time writer and use paper by the barrel, sometimes I have to be careful not to tear and/or crumble when he is in earshot. Some of my notes become extremely difficult to read when soaked in kitty saliva.

2. A PLASTIC BAG TIED IN A KNOT

This toy has been around ever since grocery stores began using plastic bags, and bless the cat lover who first thought it up. What you do to make this toy is to take a plastic grocery bag and run it through your hand until it's long and thick, like a piece of plastic material. You then tie this into a knot, approximately in the middle of the strip's length. Then tie another knot. And then another, so that the center knot keeps getting bigger and bigger until it's the size of, say, between a golf ball and one of those small round white potatoes you buy in a can. You will now have a knotted plastic ball with two tails. Cut the plastic tails so that there is about an inch of plastic on each side of the knot ball. That's it. Throw it on the floor and watch how much fun your cat has with this free toy. Note: You can also use a white plastic trash bag (the small 9 gallon size for bathroom pails works well) but since you have to pay for those, I suggest you save a few of the grocery bags you get for free so you have a ready supply of homemade toy-making materials for your feline.

3. A PAPER TOWEL OR TOILET PAPER CARDBOARD ROLL

Cats love to wrap their legs around these cardboard rolls, claw at the cardboard with their back paws, while chewing on the roll's top edge. The long paper towel rolls are good for longer cats; the toilet paper rolls work well for kittens. They roll, too.

4. A BROWN PAPER GROCERY BAG

This "toy" would not have been discovered if it wasn't common practice for many people to throw their grocery bags on the kitchen floor after emptying out the groceries. It seems to be an unbreakable rule that if a cat spots an empty brown paper grocery bag on the floor, he will, oh yes, go inside it. If the bag is on its side, you can bet your house that your kitty will run into this unexpected, yet welcome, portable cave and make himself at home. If the bag is upright, your cat will likely jump inside and peer up at you. (A recent TV cat food commercial showed a cat doing just that and it was just too damn cute for words.) A word of caution: Be careful when walking around a grocery bag on its side. There may be a cat inside it, watching the activities from his secret cavern and he will not take kindly to being stepped on or having a toddler roll over him in his walker.

5. AN EMPTY TISSUE BOX

The full-sized boxes work best for this toy. When you empty out a tissue box, do the following to it: using a razor, cut out the plastic on the top (where the tissue pops out), making a rectangular hole in the top of the box. Do the same for the long sides and the bottom of the box. (Leave the ends alone.) Your cat will have big fun sticking his paws inside the holes and tumbling around on the floor with the box. Sometimes he will get his head stuck in one of the holes and will then run around a bit with a tissue box around his neck until he figures out how to get it off. And he will figure it out, and then wreak havoc on the box for attempting to ensnare him like that. For added fun, try tossing one of the crumpled up paper toys (No. 1) into the tissue box.

85 CAT BREEDS

This is a list of all the pedigreed cat breeds and their variations.

The Cat Fanciers Association recognizes 35 cat breeds, but this is because they do not differentiate between the different variations within a breed. For instance, there are 10 different types of British Shorthairs (all of which are included on this list) but the CFA counts the British Shorthair only once.

- Abyssinian
- American Bobtail
- American Curl
- American Shorthair
- American Wirehair
- Angora
- Balinese
- Bengal
- Bi-Color Longhair
- Birman
- Black Longhair
- Blue Cream Longhair
- Blue Longhair
- Bombay
- British Bi-Color Shorthair
- British Black Shorthair
- British Colorpoint Shorthair
- British Self Shorthair
- British Shorthair
- British Smoke Shorthair
- British Spotted Shorthair
- British Tabby Shorthair
- British Tipped Shorthair
- British Tortoiseshell Shorthair
- Burmese
- Burmilla
- California Spangled
- Cameo Longhair
- Chantilly
- Chartreux
- Chinchilla Longhair

- Chocolate Longhair
- Colorpoint Longhair
- Colorpoint Shorthair
- Cornish Rex
- Cream Longhair
- Cymric
- Devon Rex
- Egyptian Mau
- European Burmese
- European Shorthair
- Exotic Shorthair
- Havana Brown
- Himalayan
- Japanese Bobtail
- Javanese
- Korat
- La Perm
- Lilac Longhair
- Maine Coon
- Malayan
- Manx
- Munchkin
- Nebelung
- Norwegian Forest
- Ocicat
- Oriental Longhair
- Oriental Shorthair

- Persian
- Pewter Longhair
- Pixie-Bob
- Ragamuffing
- Ragdoll
- Red Longhair
- Rex
- Russian
- Russian Blue
- Scottish Fold
- Selkirk Rex
- Siamese
- Siberian
- Singapura
- Smoke Longhair
- Snowshoe
- Sokoke
- Somali
- Sphynx
- Spotted Mist
- Tabby Longhair
- Tiffany
- Tonkinese
- Tortoiseshell
- Turkish Angora
- Turkish Van
- White Longhair

WHERE YOU CAN CHECK OUT THE BREEDS...

The first cat show took place in New York City in 1881 and that humble and somewhat disorganized event started a tradition that has shown no sign of slowing down. There are hundreds of cat shows each year all over the world, and there are several organizations devoted to cat show aficionados.

If you are interested in attending a cat show in your area, there are several ways of finding information about what shows are taking place and where.

HOW TO MEDICATE A CAT

Pills: You can do several things with a pill. If it's a tablet, you can crush it and mix it in with his food. If it's a capsule, you can open it and mix it in with his food. Some people use a pill gun to shoot a pill down a cat's throat but I have never been able to deal with the concept of putting a gun barrel in my cat's mouth and pulling the trigger. If you want to get the pill down your cat's throat intact, here's a technique I have found very effective. Lay kitty down on its left side on the carpet or on the seat of a chair. Use your left hand to grasp its head and place your left middle finger and left thumb at the corners of its mouth. If you press gently on these spots, kitty will often open its mouth. Then, with two fingers of your right hand, quickly place the pill in kitty's mouth as far back as you can get it, and immediately remove your fingers. Stroke kitty's throat. Usually this is all it takes, but it may require a few tries, especially if your cat freaks out somewhat by being so invaded. One caution: Do not accidentally or intentionally move your cat's jaw from side to side—the muscles of its jaws do not allow sideways movement and you can injure her.

Liquid: The best way to get liquid medicine in a cat is with a syringe. You can buy squeeze syringes with measurements on the side. Place the tip of the syringe inside the corner of the cat's mouth, hold its muzzle closed, and squeeze. The medicine will go into kitty's mouth and he will be forced to swallow it.

One of the quickest ways is to visit the Cats United International Web site at: *www.catsunited.com/html/cat_shows.html*

This organization provides an online calendar of shows that extends years into the future, as well as being a comprehensive resource for all things cat.

Cats United also provides links to the biggest cat organizations in the world, including the American Association of Cat Enthusiasts, the American Cat Fancier Association, and others. Their site also offers breed information, cat health information, and a reading room.

If you do not have a computer and you are interested in visiting this valuable site, it would well be worth your time to visit a public library and see what *catsunited.com* has to offer.

Other sources for info about cat shows are the cat magazines, including *Cat Fancy*, *Cats*, and others, all of which provide a Show Calendar in each issue, although the listing usually only covers a couple of months. These magazines are available on newsstands, or at the library, and many of them are also available online.

THE 2 SADDEST POEMS
ABOUT LOSING A CAT

*"To fear death is nothing other than
to think oneself wise when one is not."*

—Socrates

I apologize for including these two heartbreakers, but if the day comes when you need them, you'll be glad I did.

THE RAINBOW BRIDGE

This one is a classic and does provide some comfort, if taken to heart.

🐾 🐾 🐾

Just this side of heaven is a place called Rainbow Bridge. When an animal dies that has been especially close to someone here, that pet goes to Rainbow Bridge. There are meadows and hills for all our special friends so they can run and play together. There is plenty of food, water, and sunshine and our friends are warm and comfortable.

All the animals who have been ill and old are restored to health and vigor; those who were hurt or maimed are made whole and strong again, just as we remember them in our dreams of days and times gone by. The animals are happy and content, except for one small thing; they each miss someone very special to them, who had to be left behind. They all run and play together, but the day comes when one suddenly stops and looks into the distance. His bright eyes are intent; his eager body begins to quiver. Suddenly, he begins to run from the group, flying over the green grass, his legs carrying him faster and faster.

You have been spotted, and when you and your special friend finally meet, you cling together in joyous reunion, never to be parted

227

again. The happy kisses rain upon your face; your hands again caress the beloved head, and you look once more into the trusting eyes of your pet, so long gone from your life but never absent from your heart.

Then you cross the Rainbow Bridge together...

(Anonymous)

IF I SHOULD GROW FRAIL

This first person plea from a beloved pet is one of the most powerful statements for knowing when to...well, you know.

🐾 🐾 🐾

If it should be that I grow frail and weak
And pain does keep me from my sleep,
Then will you do what must be done
for this—the last battle—can't be won.
You will be sad I understand
But don't let grief then stay your hand.
For on this day, more than the rest
Your love and friendship must stand the test.
We have had so many happy years,
You wouldn't want me to suffer so.
When the time comes, please, let me go.
Take me to where my needs they'll tend,
Only, stay with me till the end.
And hold me firm and speak to me
Until my eyes no longer see.
I know in time you will agree
It is a kindness you do to me.
Although my tail its last has waved,
From pain and suffering I have been saved.
Don't grieve that it must now be you
Who has to decide this thing to do.
We've been so close—we two—these years,
Don't let your heart hold any tears.

(Author Unknown)

STEPHEN SPIGNESI'S 2 CATS, BENNIE AND CARTER

BENNIE AND CARTER

This memoir is about my two cats, Bennie and Carter, but it is also about the final days of a beloved pet and what it's like to make the decision to say goodbye for the last time. If you read this chapter in conjunction with the "2 Saddest Poems About Losing a Pet" chapter, I will not be responsible for the resulting shortage of tissues in your home.

BENNIE

Bennie Spignesi was born in July 1981 as one of a three-kitten litter while away at college. Well, actually, Bennie's mother was at college with her human, and she (the cat) gave birth in a college dorm just before the summer break of 1981.

The college girl's mother told her she could bring the three newborn kitties home with her for the summer, but that she'd have to give them away before Labor Day because she herself couldn't take care of them, and they certainly could not go back to school with her.

The girl ran an ad in the *Branford Review* and since my wife and I were looking for a kitten, I went out and took a look at them.

The three kitties were all orange and, of course, all adorable.

I pet and scratched two of them, and they each lay there contentedly purring. When I pet Bennie, though, he rolled over on his back, grabbed my hand with his four legs, and started gnawing on me like I was some kind of new chew toy delivered especially for his amusement.

"This is the guy for me," I said to College Girl, and away we went.

229

The first time I carried Bennie to the car for our inaugural car ride home together, he was small enough for me to hold in the palm of my hand. When we took our final ride together to the vet's, he had lost so much weight I was easily able to again carry him in one hand. But I'll get to that scene in a minute.

When we first brought Ben home, my wife Pam named him after one of our favorite Elton John songs, "Bennie and the Jets." I was playing piano and singing in clubs at that time and Elton was a big source of material for my "act," such as it was. One night, when I was singing "Bennie and the Jets" for my audience, I actually paid attention to the lyrics and almost fell off the piano bench when I got to the line that goes, "She's got electric boots, a mohair suit, you know I read it in a magaziiiiine."

She's got electric boots.

She.

Bennie, in Elton's song, was a girl. But by now, it was too late: Bennie had already imprinted his name onto his feline brainpan and there was no turning back. Out of respect for his masculinity, though, I shortened his name to Ben. Pam would have no part of such truncation, however. Up until the day he died, he was her "Bennie."

Bennie was a mellow cat, his childhood rambunctiousness notwithstanding. He was extraordinarily content to sleep, eat, and be stroked, and as he aged, he became the lord of the manor, regal in his bearing, dignified in his demeanor, and mostly tolerant of fools, children, and visitors.

Bennie was part of our lives and shared in—and made better—many milestone events, including the publication of my first book; our 20th wedding anniversary; and the purchase of our first home; and he always adapted to changes with a stoic (I always thought of it as bemused) acceptance.

In his 16th year, Bennie got sick.

It began with him vomiting up yellow bile and having diarrhea. He was diagnosed with kidney failure and the prescribed treatment was IV fluids (at first administered at the veterinary hospital and then by me at home) combined with Prednisone, Amphojel, and baby food fed by hand. None of this worked, and there came a day when Bennie had to lie down prostrate on the floor halfway to his litter box, such was his nausea and exhaustion from his failing kidneys, (No matter how sick he felt, he never soiled his bed or the carpet and always made it to his litter box.) By this day, his breath smelled of ammonia, he hadn't eaten anything but what I had force-fed him for weeks, and he felt like skin and bones when I picked him up.

Bennie spent his final days lying under the piano, his face to the wall, listless and quiet. The fluids I was giving him had dextrose and saline and vitamins in the IV bag and, for a time, he did feel better for a couple of days after he got a treatment, but it was a temporary fix and there really is no way of saving a cat's diseased kidneys. I was told that 76 percent of all cats over the age of 10 experience kidney failure.

He wouldn't die in pain, I was told. Kidney failure in cats causes nausea, which eliminates the appetite, and prevents the elimination of toxins from the blood via the urine, which eventually causes everything to shut down. When Ben finally needed to go on to wherever beloved pets go after they leave us, I'll help him make the trip.

The day he couldn't make it to the litter box was the day when my wife and I decided that it would be cruelty to let him go on like this. I made the call, and I took him for one last ride. I had made arrangements to leave him at the front desk with a veterinary technician I knew personally so I would not have to sit in the waiting room with him. I could not be in the room when they "put him to sleep." I left the carrier and went back for it a few days later. It still had some strands of his fur inside.

Later, I wrote this poem:

THE DRIVER

for B.

the driver walks out of his
condo's front door
slides
    into the red nova and
drives
    past the tilted no parking sign
down woodward to main
bleeding and crying
his cat just died.

the cat lies in the olive green carrier
on the seat next to him
but he is bringing him to die
one last scratch on the head
in north haven and then a

horrible
screaming
drive
home

🐾 🐾 🐾

Bennie lived 5,496 days. His pictures still hang in my study. And I think that's about all I want to say about Bennie.

🐾 🐾 🐾

Death be not proud, though some have called you
Mighty and dreadful, for, you are not so,
For, those, whom you think, you do overthrow,
Die not, poor death, nor yet can you kill me.
From rest and sleep, which but your pictures be,
Much pleasure, then from you, much more must flow,
And soon our best men with you do go,
Rest of their bones, and soul's delivery.
You are slave to Fate, Chance, kings, and desperate men,
And do with poison, war, and sickness dwell,
And poppy, or charms can make us sleep as well,
And better than your stroke; why swell you then?
One short sleep past, we wake eternally,
And death shall be no more; death, you shall die.
—John Donne

CARTER

Now we come to my current potentate of the realm, Carter Spignesi, named for my wife's and my favorite character on *ER*, Dr. John Carter.

I adopted Carter from a rescue shelter when he was about 6 weeks old. He had an eye infection which cleared up quickly with antibiotic ointment (thoughtfully provided by the woman who runs the shelter) and it wasn't long before he settled in at our house and had us trained to his specifications.

If you've already read the chapter "10 Secrets of Your Cat's Tail," you will know that one of the first things Carter did after moving in with us was break his hip.

STEPHEN SPIGNESI
Carter Spignesi.

Carter is only four years old at this writing (which is between 32 and 45 in human years, depending on which system of calculating a cat's age you choose to use—See the chapter "4 Ways To Calculate a Cat's Age") and, so far, he's been a good boy...most of the time. As I said, he did, after all, break his hip, and he has been known to knock stuff over for the sake of seeing

Carter shows off his extensive Stephen King collection.

things fall to the floor, but, overall, he's a friendly, loving, playful cat who helps me write and has eliminated all need for an alarm clock in this house, as he wakes me up at 6:30 on the dot every morning.

One thing about Carter: he will not eat cat treats or human food. I have offered him pieces of shrimp or tuna and he sniffs them, looks at me as if to say, "Why are you showing me these things?" and then turns and walks away. He is perfectly satisfied with two small cans of Triumph cat food a day, and is especially fond of their Beef and Salmon and Turkey recipes.

Right now, as I type, Carter is bathing himself on the recliner in my office. Prior to taking up residence on the chair, he ran around a little, jumped up onto the piano and then jumped off the piano; leaped up on top of a filing cabinet and then leaped down off the filing cabinet; growled at a bluejay on the tree outside my office window; drank some water; knocked some magazines off my desk; head butted me a few times; chewed on a catnip mouse; and stalked some invisible prey that was somewhere on the expanse of carpet between my desk and the etagere, all in a matter of less than three minutes, and all with an enviable commitment to action from which some of us could learn a lesson. Now he's had it up to here with the expending of energy and will now devote himself to a nap that could last anywhere from one hour to four hours. Then he will get up and do it all over again—but only after he screams at me to feed him and I obediently comply.

Cats.

You gotta love 'em.

16 CAT RETIREMENT HOMES

Just this side of heaven is a place called Rainbow Bridge...

Have you ever wondered or worried about what would happen to your beloved kitty if you yourself crossed the human Rainbow Bridge and there was no one left behind to take care of your cat?

Well, wonder no more. There are actually cat retirement homes and other programs that will be sure your cat is well cared for if left on this side of the Bridge.

These organizations and retirement homes will work with you to set up a plan for your cat if you die and you have no friends or family members who you can be confident will adopt your cat. This is a great thing. I personally know of one rescue shelter that will not adopt out a kitten to a person in their 50s because they are too worried about what would happen if the cat outlived the owner. These pre-planned retirement adoption programs take the worry out of this very real scenario.

AMERICAN SOCIETY FOR THE WELFARE OF CATS

P.O. Box 594
Alloway, NJ 08001
magic@waterw.com
catsociety.findhere.com

ANIMAL HELPLINE

P.O. Box 944
Morongo Valley, CA 92256

ASSISI ANIMAL FOUNDATION

P.O. Box 143
Crystal Lake, IL 60039-0143
assisi@ind.com

ASSOCIATED HUMANE SOCIETIES

1 Humane Way
Box 43
Forked River, NJ 08731
NJHumane@aol.com
community.nj.com/CC/HumaneSociety

BLUEBELL FOUNDATION FOR CATS

20982 Laguna Canyon Road
Laguna Beach, CA 92651
info@bluebell.org
www.bluebell.org

CAT CARE SOCIETY

5985 W. 11th Avenue
Lakewood, CO 80214
(303) 239-9680
www.catcaresociety.org

CEDARHILL ANIMAL SANCTUARY INC.

144 Sanctuary Loop
Caledonia, MS 39740

FRIENDS OF CATS INC.

P.O. Box 1613
Lakeside, CA 92040
FriendsofCatsCA@aol.com
www.friendsofcats.com

THE HERMITAGE NO-KILL CAT SHELTER

P.O. Box 13508
Tucson, AZ 85732
(520) 571-7839
www.scottnet.com/cats

THE HOPE FOR ANIMALS SANCTUARY OF RHODE ISLAND INC.

P.O. Box 816
Slatersville, RI 02876-0816

LAST CHANCE FOR LIFE

P.O. Box 13190
Oklahoma, City, OK 73113

THE LAST POST

95 Belden St.
Falls village, CT 06031
(860) 824-0831

LIVING FREE

P.O. Box 5
54250 Keen Camp Road
Mountain Center, CA 92561
(909) 659-4684
www.idyllmntn.com/livingfree/

JUDITH LaFIURA

Instead of a retirement house, Zipper the Cat spent his formative years in the Theta Xi fraternity house at Lehigh University. He currently lives a much more sedate life at Franklin Lakes, N.J.

NATIONAL CAT PROTECTION SOCIETY

P.O. Box 6218
Long Beach, CA 90806
National Cat Protection Society
6904 W. Pacific Coast Highway
Newport Beach, CA 92663

NORTH SHORE ANIMAL LEAGUE

25 Davis Ave.
Port Washington, NY 11050
NASL1@aol.com
www.NASL.org

I LOVE MY LITTLE KITTY
BY MOTHER GOOSE

I love my little kitty
And if I don't hurt her
She'll do me no harm
I won't pull her tail,
Or drive her away
And kitty and I
Very gently will play.

239

27 VETERINARY SCHOOLS, 3 WEB SITES, AND 20 HOTLINES FOR CAT LOVERS

27 COLLEGES AND UNIVERSITIES THAT OFFER DEGREES IN VETERINARY MEDICINE

For those of you interested in becoming a vet, (or if you know someone who is leaning towards a career as a veterinarian), these schools all offer degrees in veterinary medicine. I have provided their mailing info, and following this listing of schools are a few Web resources to access information about colleges and universities. Also, for a complete listing of all veterinary schools in the United States, organized by state, check out these informative Web sites:

- *www.avma.org/care4pets/educvcol.htm*
- *www.montana.edu/wwwvmbl/ugradprog/prevet/usschools.html*
- *vetmedicine.about.com/health/vetmedicine/cs/schools/*
- *www.colorado.edu/ArtsSciences/aacforstudents/pre_pro/vetschools.htm*

AUBURN UNIVERSITY

College of Veterinary Medicine
180 Greene Hall
Auburn University, AL 36489

UNIVERSITY OF CALIFORNIA AT DAVIS

School of Veterinary Medicine
Dean's Office
1 Shields Avenue
Davis, CA 95616

COLORADO STATE UNIVERSITY

College of Veterinary Medicine and Biomedical Sciences
W102 Anatomy Building
Fort Collins, CO 80523-1601

CORNELL UNIVERSITY

Cornell University College of Veterinary Medicine
180 Greene Hall
Ithaca, NY 14853-6401

UNIVERSITY OF FLORIDA

College of Veterinary Medicine
P.O. Box 100125
Gainesville, FL 32610-0125

UNIVERSITY OF GEORGIA

College of Veterinary Medicine
Athens, GA 30602

UNIVERSITY OF ILLINOIS

College of Veterinary Medicine
2001 South Lincoln
Urbana, IL 61802

IOWA STATE UNIVERSITY

College of Veterinary Medicine
Ames, IA 50011-1250

KANSAS STATE UNIVERSITY

College of Veterinary Medicine
Trotter Hall
Room 101
Manhattan, KS 66506-0117

LOUISIANA STATE UNIVERSITY

School of Veterinary Medicine
S. Stadium Drive
Baton Rouge, LA 70803

MICHIGAN STATE UNIVERSITY

College of Veterinary Medicine
A-120E East Fee Hall
East Lansing, MI 48824-1316

UNIVERSITY OF MINNESOTA

College of Veterinary Medicine
1365 Gortner Avenue
St. Paul, MN 55108

MISSISSIPPI STATE UNIVERSITY

College of Veterinary Medicine
P.O. Box 9825
Mississippi State, MS 39762

UNIVERSITY OF MISSOURI

College of Veterinary Medicine
W. 203 Veterinarian Medical Building
Columbia, MO 65211

NORTH CAROLINA STATE UNIVERSITY

College of Veterinary Medicine
4700 Hillsborough Street
Raleigh, NC 27606-1499

OHIO STATE UNIVERSITY

College of Veterinary Medicine
101 Sisson Hall
1900 Coffey Road
Columbus, OH 43210

OKLAHOMA STATE UNIVERSITY

College of Veterinary Medicine
Stillwater, OK 74078-2005

OREGON STATE UNIVERSITY

College of Veterinary Medicine
200 Magruder Hall
Corvallis, OR 97331-4801

UNIVERSITY OF PENNSYLVANIA

School of Veterinary Medicine
3800 Spruce Street
Philadelphia, PA 19104-6047

PURDUE UNIVERSITY

School of Veterinary Medicine
1240 Lynn Hall
West Lafayette, IN 47907-1240

UNIVERSITY OF TENNESSEE

College of Veterinary Medicine
P.O. Box 1071
Knoxville, TN 37901-1071

TEXAS A&M UNIVERSITY

College of Veterinary Medicine
College Station, TX 77843-4461

TUFTS UNIVERSITY

School of Veterinary Medicine
200 Westboro Road
North Grafton, MA 01536

TUSKEGEE UNIVERSITY

School of Veterinary Medicine
Patterson Hall
Tuskegee, AL 36088

VIRGINIA TECH

Virginia-Maryland Regional College of Veterinary Medicine
Blacksburg, VA 24061-0443

WASHINGTON STATE UNIVERSITY

College of Veterinary Medicine
Pullman, WA 99164-7010

UNIVERSITY OF WISCONSIN

School of Veterinary Medicine
2015 Linden Drive W.
Madison, WI 53706-1102

WEB RESOURCES FOR THE VETERINARY SCHOOL-BOUND

COLLEGE OPPORTUNITIES ON-LINE (COOL)

nces.ed.gov/ipeds/cool/
COOL is a direct link to over 9,000 colleges and universities in the United States.

COLLEGE-SCHOLARSHIPS.COM

www.college-scholarships.com/
This site, organized by state, compiles contact information for United States universities and scholarship offices, with e-mail addresses, phone numbers, and snail mail info, and more.

DEGREE SEARCH

www.degreesearch.com
This site allows you to search for specific degree programs and provides profiles of over 8,000 United States colleges or universities.

19 CAT HOT LINES

These hot lines provide information about feline health and behavior, grief counseling and pet loss support, and poison control information. Some are toll-free; some are long distance calls for which you, the caller, pay all fees. When a fee-for-service is required, the latest pricing information is provided. (I have not provided pet products company's hot line numbers. These numbers are usually provided as part of the company's packaging information.)

- Animal Behavior Helpline: (415) 554-3075.
- Chicago Veterinary Medical Association Pet Loss Support Hot Line: (630) 603-3994. Leave a message; they'll usually call you back that evening.
- Colorado State University Pet Loss Support Hot Line: (970) 491-1242.
- Dial-A-Vet: (800) 719-8916. $19 for the first 10 minutes, $2 for each additional minute.
- Dr. Louis J. Camuti Memorial Feline Consultation and Diagnostic Service: (800) 548-8937. Consultation fee by credit card.
- Iowa State University Pet Loss Support Hot Line: (888) 478-7574.
- Lyme Disease National Hot Line: (800) 886-5963.
- Michigan State University Pet Loss Support Hotline: (517) 432-2696. Leave a message; they'll usually call you back that evening.
- National Animal Poison Control Center (American Society for the Prevention of Cruelty to Animals): (800) 548-2423 or (900) 680-000. $45 per case.
- Ohio State University Pet Loss Support Hot Line: (614) 292-1823.
- Pet Loss Support Hot Line: (607) 253-3932. Leave a message; they'll usually call you back that evening.
- Tree House Animal Foundation: (773) 506-3235. Feline information
- Tufts University School of Veterinary Medicine Pet Loss Support Hot Line: (508) 839-7966.
- University of California at Davis Pet Loss Support Hot Line: (530) 752-4200.
- University of Florida at Gainesville Pet Loss Support Hot Line: (352) 392-4700, ext. 4080.
- University of Illinois, Urbana Pet Loss Support Hot Line: (217) 244-2273. Leave a message; they'll usually call you back that evening.
- University of Pennsylvania Pet Loss Support Hot Line: (215) 898-4529.
- Virginia-Maryland Regional College of Veterinary Medicine Pet Loss Support Hot Line: (540) 231-8038.
- Washington State University Pet Loss Support Hot Line: (509) 335-5704.

"THE CAT THAT WALKED BY HIMSELF" BY RUDYARD KIPLING

Ever wonder why cats are such loners and so independent? This charming 1902 classic short story by Rudyard Kipling explains how dogs, horses, and cows came to be tamed by man during the time when we lived in caves, but cats refused to be dominated and have insisted on walking by themselves ever since.

Originally published in Kipling's *Just So Stories*, this fable puts a mythic spin on the development of the cat's personality and illustrates why the feline continues to walk "by his wild lone."

🐾 🐾 🐾

Hear and attend and listen; for this befell and behappened and became and was, O my Best Beloved, when the Tame animals were wild. The Dog was wild, and the Horse was wild, and the Cow was wild, and the Sheep was wild, and the Pig was wild—as wild as wild could be—and they walked in the Wet Wild Woods by their wild lones. But the wildest of all wild animals was the Cat. He walked by himself, and all places were alike to him.

Of course the Man was wild too. He was dreadfully wild. He didn't even begin to be tame till he met the Woman, and she told him that she did not like living in his wild ways. She picked out a nice dry Cave, instead of a heap of wet leaves, to lie down in; and she lit a nice fire of wood at the back of the Cave; and she hung a dried wild-horse skin, tail-down, across the opening of the Cave; and she said, "Wipe your feet, dear, when you come in, and now we'll keep house."

That night, Best Beloved, they ate wild sheep roasted on the hot stones, and flavoured with wild garlic and wild pepper; and wild duck stuffed with wild rice and wild fenugreek and wild coriander; and marrow-bones of wild oxen; and wild cherries and wild grenadillas. Then the Man went to sleep in the front of the fire ever so happy;

247

but the Woman sat up, combing her hair. She took the bone of the shoulder of mutton—the big fat blade-bone—and she looked at the wonderful marks on it, and she threw more wood on the fire, and she made a Magic. She made the First Singing Magic in the world.

Out in the Wet Wild Woods all the wild animals gathered together where they could see the light of the fire a long way off, and they wondered what it meant.

Then Wild Horse stamped with his wild foot and said, "O my Friends and O my Enemies, why have the Man and the Woman made that great light in that great Cave, and what harm will it do us?"

Wild Dog lifted up his wild nose and smelled the smell of roast mutton, and said: "I will go and see and look, and say; for I think it is good. Cat, come with me."

"Nenni!" said the Cat. "I am the Cat who walks by himself, and all places are alike to me. I will not come."

"Then we can never be friends again," said Wild Dog, and he trotted off to the Cave. But when he had gone a little way the Cat said to himself, "All places are alike to me. Why should I not go and see and look and come away at my own liking." So he slipped after Wild Dog softly, very softly, and hid himself where he could hear everything.

When Wild Dog reached the mouth of the Cave he lifted up the dried horse-skin with his nose and sniffed the beautiful smell of the roast mutton, and the Woman, looking at the blade-bone, heard him, and laughed, and said, "Here comes the first. Wild Thing out of the Wild Woods, what do you want?"

Wild Dog said, "O my Enemy and Wife of my Enemy, what is this that smells so good in the Wild Woods?"

Then the Woman picked up a roasted mutton-bone and threw it to Wild Dog, and said, "Wild Thing out of the Wild Woods, taste and try." Wild Dog gnawed the bone, and it was more delicious than anything he had ever tasted, and he said, "O, my Enemy and Wife of my Enemy, give me another."

The Woman said, "Wild Thing out of the Wild Woods, help my Man to hunt through the day and guard his Cave at night, and I will give you as many roast bones as you need."

"Ah!" said the Cat, listening. "This is a very wise Woman, but she is not so wise as I am."

Wild Dog crawled into the Cave and laid his head on the Woman's lap, and said, "O my Friend and Wife of my Friend, I will help your Man to hunt through the day, and at night I will guard your Cave."

"Ah!" said the Cat, listening. "That is a very foolish Dog." And he went back through the Wet Wild Woods waving his wild tail, and walking by his wild lone. But he never told anybody.

When the Man waked up he said, "What is Wild Dog doing here?" And the Woman said, "His name is not Wild Dog anymore, but the First Friend, because he will be our friend for always and always and always. Take him with you when you go hunting."

Next night the Woman cut great green armsful of fresh grass from the water-meadows, and dried it before the fire, so that it smelt like new-mown hay, and she sat at the mouth of the Cave and plaited a halter out of horse-hide, and she looked at the shoulder of mutton-bone—at the big broad blade-bone—and she made a Magic. She made the Second Singing Magic in the world.

Out in the Wild Woods all the wild animals wondered what had happened to Wild Dog, and at last Wild Horse stamped with his foot and said, "I will go and see and say why Wild Dog has not returned. Cat, come with me."

"Nenni!" said the Cat. "I am the Cat who walks by himself, and all places are alike to me. I will not come." But all the same he followed Wild Horse softly, very softly, and hid himself where he could hear everything.

When the Woman heard Wild Horse tripping and stumbling on his long mane, she laughed and said, "Here comes the second. Wild thing out of the Wild Woods, what do you want?"

Wild Horse said, "O my Enemy and Wife of my Enemy, where is Wild Dog?"

The Woman laughed, picked up the blade-bone and looked at it, and said, "Wild Thing out of the Wild Woods, you did not come here for Wild Dog, but for the sake of this good grass."

And Wild Horse, tripping and stumbling on his long mane, said, "That is true; give it me to eat."

The Woman said, "Wild Thing out of the Wild Woods, bend your wild head and wear what I give you, and you shall eat the wonderful grass three times a day."

"Ah," said the Cat, listening, "this is a clever woman, but she is not so clever as I am."

Wild Horse bent his wild head, and the Woman slipped the plaited hide halter over it, and said, "O my Mistress, and Wife of my Master, I will be your servant for the sake of the wonderful grass."

"Ah," said the Cat, listening, "that is a very foolish Horse." And he went back through the Wet Wild Woods, waving his tail and walking by his wild lone. But he never told anybody.

When the Man and the Dog came back from hunting, the Man said, "What is Wild Horse doing here?" And the Woman said, "His name is not Wild Horse any more, but the First Servant, because he will carry us from place to place for always and always and always. Ride on his back when you go hunting."

Next day, holding her wild head high that her wild horns should not catch in the wild trees, Wild Cow came up to the Cave, and the Cat followed, and hid himself just the same as before; and everything happened just the same as before; and the Cat said the same things as before, and when Wild Cow had promised to give her milk to the Woman every day in exchange for the wonderful grass, the Cat went back through the Wet Wild Woods waving his wild tail and walking by his wild lone, just the same as before. But he never told anybody. And when the Man and the Horse and the Dog came home from hunting and asked the same questions same as before, the Woman said, "Her name is not Wild Cow anymore, but the Giver of Good Food. She will give us the warm white milk for always and always and always, and I will take care of her while you and the First Friend and the First Servant go hunting."

Next day the Cat waited to see if any other Wild thing would go up to the Cave, but no one moved in the Wet Wild Woods, so the Cat walked there by himself; and he saw the Woman milking the Cow, and he saw the light of the fire in the Cave, and he smelt the smell of the warm white milk.

Cat said, "O my Enemy and Wife of my Enemy, where did Wild Cow go?"

The Woman laughed and said, "Wild Thing out of the Wild Woods, go back to the Woods again, for I have braided up my hair, and I have put away the magic blade-bone, and we have no more need of either friends or servants in our Cave."

Cat said, "I am not a friend, and I am not a servant. I am the Cat who walks by himself, and I wish to come into your cave."

Woman said, "Then why did you not come with First Friend on the first night?"

Cat grew very angry and said, "Has Wild Dog told tales of me?"

Then the Woman laughed and said, "You are the Cat who walks by himself, and all places are alike to you. You are neither a friend nor a servant. You have said it yourself. Go away and walk by yourself in all places alike."

Then Cat pretended to be sorry and said, "Must I never come into the Cave? Must I never sit by the warm fire? Must I never drink the white milk? You are very wise and very beautiful. You should not be cruel even to a Cat."

Woman said, "I knew I was wise, but I did not know I was beautiful. So I will make a bargain with you. If I ever say one word in your praise you may come into the Cave."

"And if you say two words in my praise?" said the Cat.

"I never shall," said the Woman, "but if I say two words in your praise you may sit by the fire in the Cave."

"And if you say three words?" said the Cat.

"I never shall," said the Woman, "but if I say three words in your praise you may drink the warm white milk three times a day for always and always and always."

Then the Cat arched his back and said, "Now let the Curtain at the mouth of the Cave, and the Fire at the back of the Cave, and the Milk-pots that stand beside the Fire, remember what my Enemy and the Wife of my Enemy has said." And he went away through the Wet Wild Woods waving his wild tail and walking by his wild lone.

That night when the Man and the Horse and the Dog came home from hunting, the woman did not tell them of the bargain that she had made with the Cat, because she was afraid that they might not like it.

Cat went far and far away and hid himself in the Wet Wild Woods by his wild lone for a long time till the Woman forgot all about him. Only the Bat—the little upside-down Bat—that hung inside the Cave, knew where Cat hid; and every evening Bat would fly to Cat with news of what was happening.

WENDY GREENWALD

Abby: The cat that washed by herself in the sink.

One evening Bat said, "There is a Baby in the Cave. He is new and pink and fat and small, and the Woman is very fond of him."

"Ah," said the Cat, listening, but what is the Baby fond of?"

"He is fond of things that are soft and tickle," said the Bat. "He is fond of warm things to hold in his arms when he goes to sleep. He is fond of being played with. He is fond of all these things."

"Ah," said the Cat, listening, "then my time has come."

Next night Cat walked through the Wet Wild Woods and hid very near the Cave till morning-time, and Man and Dog and Horse went hunting. The Woman was busy cooking that morning, and the Baby cried and interrupted. So she carried him outside the Cave and gave him a handful of pebbles to play with. But still the Baby cried.

Then the Cat put out his paddy paw and patted the Baby on the cheek, and it cooed; and the Cat rubbed against its fat knees and tickled under its fat chin with his tail. And the Baby laughed and the Woman heard him and smiled.

Then the Bat—the little upside-down Bat—that hung in the mouth of the Cave said, "O my Hostess and Wife of my Host and Mother of my Host's Son, a Wild Thing from the Wild Woods is most beautifully playing with your Baby."

"A blessing on that Wild Thing whoever he may be," said the Woman, straightening her back, "for I was a busy woman this morning and he has done me a service."

The very minute and second, Best Beloved, the dried horse-skin Curtain that was stretched tail-down at the mouth of the Cave fell down—woosh!—because it remembered the bargain she had made with the Cat, and when the Woman went to pick it up—lo and behold!—the Cat was sitting quite comfy inside the Cave.

"O my Enemy and Wife of my Enemy and Mother of my Enemy," said the Cat, "it is I, for you have spoken a word in my praise, and now I can sit within the Cave for always and always and always. But still I am the Cat who walks by himself, and all places are alike to me."

The woman was very angry, and shut her lips tight and took up her spinning-wheel and began to spin.

But the Baby cried because the Cat had gone away, and the Woman could not hush it, for it struggled and kicked and grew black in the face.

"O my Enemy and Wife of my Enemy and Mother of my Enemy," said the Cat, "take a strand of the wire that you are spinning and tie it to your spinning-whorl and drag it along the floor, and I will show you a magic that shall make your Baby laugh as loudly as he is now crying."

"I will do so," said the Woman, "because I am at my wits' end; but I will not thank you for it."

She tied the thread to the little clay spindle-wheel and drew it across the floor, and the Cat ran after it and patted it with his paws and rolled head over heels, and tossed it backwards over his shoulder and chased it between his hind-legs and pretended to lose it, and pounced down upon it again, till the Baby laughed as loudly as it had been crying, and scrambled after the Cat and frolicked all over the Cave till it grew tired and settled down to sleep with the Cat in its arms.

"Now," said the Cat, "I will sing the Baby a song that shall keep him asleep for an hour." And he began to purr, loud and low, low and loud, till the Baby fell fast asleep. The Woman smiled as she looked down upon the two of them and said, "That was wonderfully done. No question but you are very clever, O Cat."

That very minute and second, Best Beloved, the smoke of the fire at the back of the Cave came down in clouds from the roof—puff!—because it remembered the bargain she had made with the Cat, and when it had cleared away—lo and behold!—the Cat was sitting quite comfy close to the fire.

"O my Enemy and Wife of my Enemy and Mother of my Enemy," said the Cat, "it is I, for you have spoken a second word in my praise, and now I can sit by the warm fire at the back of the Cave for always and always and always. But still I am the Cat who walks by himself, and all places are alike to me."

Then the Woman was very very angry, and let down her hair and put more wood on the fire and brought out the broad blade-bone of the shoulder of mutton and began to make a Magic that should prevent her from saying a third word in praise of the Cat. It was not a singing Magic, Best Beloved, it was a Still Magic; and by and by the Cave grew so still that a little wee-wee mouse crept out of a corner and ran across the floor.

"O my Enemy and Wife of my Enemy and Mother of my Enemy," said the Cat, "is that little mouse part of your magic?"

"Ouh! Chee! No indeed!" said the Woman, and she dropped the blade-bone and jumped upon the footstool in front of the fire and braided up her hair very quick for fear that the mouse should run up it.

"Ah," said the Cat, watching, "then the mouse will do me no harm if I eat it?"

"No," said the Woman, braiding up her hair, "eat it quickly and I will ever be grateful to you."

Cat made one jump and caught the little mouse, and the Woman said, "A hundred thanks. Even the First Friend is not quick enough to catch little mice as you have done. You must be very wise."

That very moment and second, O Best Beloved, the Milk-pot that stood by the fire cracked in two pieces—ffft—because it remembered the bargain she had made with the Cat, and when the Woman jumped down from the footstool—lo and behold!—the Cat was lapping up the warm white milk that lay in one of the broken pieces.

"O my Enemy and Wife of my Enemy and Mother of my Enemy," said the Cat, "it is I; for you have spoken three words in my praise, and now I can drink the warm white milk three times a day for always and always and always. But still I am the Cat who walks by himself, and all places are alike to me."

Then the Woman laughed and set the Cat a bowl of the warm white milk and said, "O Cat, you are as clever as a man, but remember that your bargain was not made with the Man or the Dog, and I do not know what they will do when they come home."

"What is that to me?" said the Cat. "If I have my place in the Cave by the fire and my warm white milk three times a day I do not care what the Man or the Dog can do."

That evening when the Man and the Dog came into the Cave, the Woman told them all the story of the bargain while the Cat sat by the fire and smiled. Then that Man said, "Yes, but he has not made a bargain with me or with all proper Men after me." Then he took off his two leather boots and he took up his little stone axe (that makes three) and he fetched a piece of wood and a hatchet (that is five altogether), and he set them out in a row and he said, "Now we will make our bargain. If you do not catch mice when you are in the Cave for always and always and always, I will throw these five things at you whenever I see you, and so shall all proper Men do after me."

"Ah," said the Woman, listening, "this is a very clever Cat, but he is not so clever as my Man."

The Cat counted the five things (and they looked very knobby) and he said, "I will catch mice when I am in the Cave for always and always and always; but still I am the Cat who walks by himself, and all places are alike to me."

"Not when I am near," said the Man, "If you had not said that last I would have put all these things away for always and always and always; but I am now going to throw my boots and my little stone axe (that makes three) at you whenever I meet you. And so shall all proper Men do after me."

Then the Dog said, "Wait a minute. He has not made a bargain with me or with all proper Dogs after me." And he showed his teeth and said, "If you are not kind to the Baby while I am in the Cave for always and always and always, I will hunt you till I catch you, and when I catch you I will bite you. And so shall all proper Dogs do after me."

"Ah," said the Woman, listening, "this is a very clever Cat, but he is not so clever as the Dog."

The Cat counted the Dog's teeth (and they looked very pointed) and he said, "I will be kind to the Baby while I am in the Cave, as long as he does not pull my tail too hard, for always and always and always; but still I am the Cat who walks by himself, and all places are alike to me."

"Not when I am near," said the Dog, "If you had not said that last I would shut my mouth for always and always and always; but now I am going to hunt you up a tree whenever I meet you. And so shall all proper Dogs do after me."

Then the Man threw his two boots and his little stone axe (that makes three) at the Cat, and the Cat ran out of the Cave and the Dog chased him up a tree; and from that day to this, Best Beloved, three proper Men out of five will always throw things at a Cat whenever they meet him, and all proper Dogs will chase him up a tree. But the Cat keeps his side of the bargain too. He will kill mice and he will be kind to Babies when he is in the house, just as long as they don't pull his tail too hard. But when he has done that, and between times, and when the moon gets up and night comes, he is the Cat that walks by himself, and all places are alike to him. Then he goes out to the Wet Wild Woods or up the Wet Wild Trees or on the Wet Wild Roofs, waving his wild tail and walking by his wild lone.

36 QUOTATIONS ABOUT CATS

For centuries, cat fanciers have had quite a bit to say about the feline population. Here are a handful of some particularly pithy remarks.

- As every cat owner knows, nobody owns a cat. (Ellen Perry Berkeley)
- Because of [the] difference between domestic cats and domestic dogs, cat lovers tend to be rather different from dog lovers. As a rule they have a stronger personality bias toward independent thought and action. Artists like cats; soldiers like dogs. (Desmond Morris)
- A cat is a cat. (Spanish proverb)
- A cat is never vulgar. (Carl Van Vechten)
- A cat is nobody's fool. (Heywood Broun)
- The cat is the individualist, the aberrant; he is the creature who has never run in packs nor fought in herds nor thought in congregations. He has the dignity of the self-contained and the confidence of the self-sufficient. If, looking at a cat, one knows for the instant some envious admiration of the unhumanly free, this is no more than momentary nostalgia, and nostalgia for a dream. It should not be blamed upon the cat. (Frances and Richard Lockridge)
- A cat is witty, he has nerve, he knows how to do precisely the right thing at the right moment. He is impulsive and facetious and appreciates the value of a well-turned pleasantry. He extricates himself from the most difficult situations by a little pirouette. To how many timid and hesitating persons could he give useful lessons. I have never seen him embarrassed. With an astounding

promptitude, he chooses instantly between two solutions of a problem, not merely that which is better from his point of view and in conformity with his interests, but also that which is elegant and gracious. (M. Poincaré)

- The cat is, above all things, a dramatist. (Margaret Benson)

- Cats accommodate and are companions to people who, in turn, provide services; thus the cat fulfills a role it neither intends nor was intended to fulfill, and the now-ancient and ongoing partnership continues, through every generation, to be freshly rewarding. (Otto Penzler)

- Cats are absolute individuals, with their own ideas about everything, including the people they own. (John Dingman)

- Cats are intended to teach us that not everything in nature has a function. (Garrison Keiller)

- Cats are not people. It's important to stress that, because excessive cat watching often leads to the delusion that cats are people. (Dan Greenburg)

- Cats have a contempt of speech. Why should they talk when they can communicate without words? (Lillian Jackson Braun)

- Cats have intercepted my footsteps at the ankle for so long that my gait, both at home and on tour, has been compared to that of a man wading through low surf. (Roy Blount Jr.)

- Cats, like men, are flatterers. (William Landor)

- A dog is a dog, a bird is a bird, and a cat is a person. (Mugsy Peabody)

- Every cat is really the most beautiful woman in the room. (E. V. Lucas)

- Her function is to sit and be admired. (Georgina Strickland Gates)

- I firmly believe that a cat does humans a favor by allowing itself to be "owned" by us. The benefits we reap from daily interaction with such a splendid animal far outweigh the costs to us, and we had better be careful cats do not discover this for themselves, or they may end up demanding a pay raise. (Stephen Spignesi)

- I love cats because I enjoy my home; and little by little, they becomes its visible soul. (Jean Cocteau)

- I value in the cat the independent and almost ungrateful spirit which prevents her from attaching herself to any one, the indifference with which she passes from the salon to the housetop. When we caress her, she stretches herself, and arches her back responsively; but that is because she feels an agreeable sensation, not because she feels a silly satisfaction, like the dog, in faithfully loving a thankless master. The cat lives alone, has no need of society, obeys only when she pleases, pretends to sleep that she may see the more clearly, and scratches everything on which she can lay her paw. (Chateaubriand)

✔ It's very hard to be polite if you're a cat. (Anonymous)

✔ The majority of cat people, deep down, have a sneaking and half-recognized suspicion that they have been taken over by their feline, four-footed friend and that to a considerable extent she has imposed her whims and wishes upon the household. (Paul Gallico)

✔ Of all domestic animals the cat is the most expressive. His face is capable of showing a wide range of expressions. His tail is a mirror of his mind. His gracefulness is surpassed only by his agility. And, along with all these, he has a sense of humor. (Walter Chandoha)

✔ One cat just leads to another. (Ernest Hemingway)

✔ The phrase "domestic cat" is an oxymoron. (George Will)

✔ The smallest feline is a masterpiece. (Leonardo Da Vinci)

✔ There are no ordinary cats. (Colette)

✔ There is no evidence that at any time during its history, the cat's way of life and its reception into human homesteads were purposely planned and directed by humans, as was the case with all other domestic animals, at least from a very early stage of their domestication...In other words, there was no agent domesticating the cat besides the cat himself. (Paul Layhausen)

ROBERT M. BRINK

Maceo says, "Leave me alone—I'm sleeping."

✔ There is not a man living who knows better than I that the four charms of a cat lie in its closed eyes, its long and lovely hair, its silence, and even its affected love. (Hilaire Belloc)

✔ There is some truth to the assertion that the cat, with the exception of a few luxury breeds...is no domestic animal but a completely wild being. (Konrad Lorenz)

✔ They're the most graceful, sinuous, sexy, truly sensuous creatures in the world. (Carol Lawrence)

✔ To understand a cat, you must realize that he has his own gifts, his own viewpoint, even his own morality. (Lillian Jackson Braun)

- When a Cat adopts you there is nothing to be done about it except to put up with it and wait until the wind changes. (T. S. Eliot)
- With their qualities of cleanliness, discretion, affection, patience, dignity, and courage, how many of us, I ask you, would be capable of being cats. (Fernand Mery)
- You can't own a cat. The best you can do is be partners. (Sir Harry Swanson)

INDEX

ABOUT THE AUTHOR

Stephen J. Spignesi is a fulltime writer who specializes in popular culture subjects, including historical biography, television, film, American and world history, and contemporary fiction.

Spignesi—christened "the world's leading authority on Stephen King" by Entertainment Weekly magazine—has written many authorized entertainment books and has worked with Stephen King, Turner Entertainment, the Margaret Mitchell Estate, Andy Griffith, Viacom, and other entertainment industry personalities and entities on a wide range of projects. Mr. Spignesi has also contributed essays, chapters, articles, and introductions to a wide range of books.

Spignesi's 30 books have been translated into several languages and he has also written for *Harper's*, *Cinefantastique*, *Saturday Review*, *Mystery Scene*, *Gauntlet*, and *Midnight Graffiti* magazines; as well as the *New York Times*, the *New York Daily News*, the *New York Post*, the *New Haven Register*, the French literary journal *Tenébres*, and the Italian online literary journal, *Horror.It*. Spignesi has also appeared on CNN, MSNBC, Fox News Channel, and other TV and radio outlets; and also appeared in the 1998 E! documentary, *The Kennedys: Power, Seduction, and Hollywood*, as a Kennedy family authority; and in the A and E *Biography* of Stephen King that aired in January 2000. Spignesi's 1997 book, *JFK Jr.*, was a *New York Times* bestseller. Mr. Spignesi's *Complete Stephen King Encyclopedia* was a 1991 Bram Stoker Award nominee.

In addition to writing, Spignesi also lectures on a variety of popular culture and historical subjects and teaches writing in the Connecticut area. He is the founder and Editor-in-Chief of the small press publishing company, The Stephen John Press, which recently published the acclaimed feminist autobiography *Open Windows*.

Spignesi is a graduate of the University of New Haven, and lives in New Haven, CT, with his wife, Pam, and their cat, Carter, named for their favorite character on ER.